— HE WON'T KNOW —

it's Paleo

100+ AUTOIMMUNE PROTOCOL RECIPES TO
Create with Love & Share with Pride

Bre'anna D. Emmitt

This book can be purchased in bulk at a discounted rate. Please contact: contact@hewontknowitspaleo.com

Photography by Bre'anna D. Emmitt and Josh Huskin, www.joshhuskin.com
Book Design by Jennifer Hicks, www.jenniferhicks.me

ISBN-10: 0692379940
ISBN-13: 978-0692379943

Disclaimer: The content in this book is for entertainment and inspiration purposes only. The author of this cookbook is not a medical professional and is not responsible for any adverse effects that may result from this book. Always speak to a qualified healthcare professional before making any changes in diet or lifestyle.

Table of Contents

To Chris, the "He" in *He Won't Know It's Paleo,*
and our three (soon-to-be four) children.
You five are the world to me.

Foreword

Transforming one's health through lifestyle change is not only possible, it is absolutely necessary to our wellness and vitality. Proper nutrition, exercise, sleep and stress management are the foundations of well-being. But what do we do when the foods we eat make us sick? Where do we look for answers? And what do we do when traditional medicine fails us? Bre'anna Emmitt is a brave soul who took matters into her own hands to find help for herself. What she discovered is the healing power of food.

Autoimmune disease is a major health problem in the United States today, affecting up to 23 million people, with direct health care costs of an estimated $100 billion. The other leading causes of death and disability are heart disease and cancer. What do they all have in common? Inflammation.

Research points toward gut health and the foods we eat as key contributors to the inflammatory process in the body. How we use this information for treatment is a big paradigm shift for many physicians, myself included.

As a board certified family medicine physician in practice for twenty years, my experiences with many different kinds of patients have been interesting, rewarding, and many times frustrating. I received little to no nutritional instruction in medical school, and so had few other tools besides prescription medications to help patients deal with their diabetes, high blood pressure, high cholesterol, migraine headaches, irritable bowel syndrome, chronic pain and other illnesses. I knew that food choices and stress management were important, but was taught to give medicines first, and refer people to a nurse or nutritionist for education.

Every day I see patients with chronic issues who are suffering. Their medications do not always help them, and in many instances are causing more harm than good. They are looking for a new way forward, and are in need of information and tools to achieve long-lasting lifestyle change which in turn will improve their function and relieve their suffering. Is this really possible? Yes, but it takes dedication, planning, encouragement and support. Bre'anna's journey is a success story, one of many I have witnessed.

Faced with her own health challenges, Bre'anna has taken her passion for cooking and worked magic in the kitchen to create nourishing and delectable recipes that have restored her health and wellbeing, while satisfying the taste buds (and likely, the health) of her family.

As a physician and working mother, I applaud Bre'anna's efforts to share her story, her experience and her recipes with all of you. I hope you will find inspiration and healing in this book.

To Your Good Health!

Simone L Norris, MD

About this Cookbook

This cookbook is dedicated to my ever-loving husband, Chris, who I knew would not enjoy switching to a paleo diet. So to make the switch successfully, I did what any good wife would do — I didn't tell him we were eating paleo for the first six months. In that time, he lost weight and commented on how great he felt, and I knew he loved the food. I finally decided it was time he knew the truth. When I told him, he laughed in disbelief and encouraged me to start a blog to post my recipes. With that, *He Won't Know It's Paleo* was born.

When I started my blog, I wasn't sure anyone would read it, so I resolved that if no one came in the first two weeks, I'd shut it down. Imagine my surprise when I had 640 views on my first day! Just a few weeks later, it was up to over a thousand per day, and needless to say, it only grew from there.

A few months in, again with Chris's encouragement, I decided to start compiling recipes for a paleo cookbook completely dedicated to the Autoimmune Protocol. After months of recipe developing, writing, editing, photographing, and planning, I am so happy to present this book to you, my faithful followers and supporters! I hope these recipes provide you with delicious meals and treats to help make this diet achievable, practical, and enjoyable!

My Story

In 2013, I sat perplexed as my ongoing digestion issues returned with a vengeance. I had experienced these issues since college, but now they were worse than ever before. With them came a lovely dose of exhaustion, hair loss, an ongoing rash that simultaneously itched and burned, sores that relentlessly populated the inside of my mouth, painful joints and spine, muscle spasms, and nerve pain and tingling.

As stupid as this now sounds, for a while I thought I was just getting older: I had three children in four years, was pushing thirty, and certainly wasn't a kid anymore. During this time, I remember looking at people in their forties and fifties and thinking, 'They must be so miserable and in so much pain all the time. Here I am not even thirty, and I feel like I'm falling apart.'

After a while, however, my symptoms progressed, and I knew it was more than just getting older. After far too many fruitless doctor appointments, I thought back to two years prior, when I'd had my last relatively symptom-free period: It was when I was pregnant and nursing our second child. After I weaned him in 2010, however, my symptoms returned and, again, left me in multiple doctors' offices searching for answers. (I later found out that autoimmune diseases often go into remission during pregnancy and breastfeeding, which explained my "breaks" in symptoms.) It was during this time I found out I had Hashimoto's thyroid disease. I remember sitting in my endocrinologist's office as she looked over my blood work and said to me, "I think you have celiac disease. You are a classic case. The easiest way to find out from here is to eat gluten-free for three weeks and see if you feel better." I did what she said and didn't feel much difference, so I started eating gluten again.

Fast forward to 2013 and I was trying to figure out my problems yet again. Again it was when I weaned our daughter that the problems rapidly worsened. Thinking back to my endocrinologist's suspicions, I started reading about the far-reaching symptoms of celiac disease and became certain it was what I had. I talked with my family doctor and resolved to eat strictly gluten-free for six weeks. Around week four, I started noticing improvement. At week five, I felt good. At week six, I felt amazing! I went in to report to my family doctor, asking her what I should do from here. She recommended that I eat gluten again—a lot of it—to be formally tested for celiac disease. Within four days, I had redeveloped every single symptom (and then some), proving it really was all connected. I called my doctor, telling her how awful I felt. Not knowing it at the time, I was beginning the worst flare up of my life. I began having strange fainting and neurological episodes and ending up spending three days in the hospital. All of the doctors I saw told me it was too dangerous for me to do a gluten challenge for celiac testing. They told me to stop eating gluten permanently, giving me a celiac diagnosis by exclusion. At first the nonofficial diagnosis really bothered me, but I realized I would never put my body through that again just to find out what seemed so obvious.

I was never able to recover from that flare just by staying gluten free. After a few months, I found a great Functional Medicine doctor and cut out dairy. Then I "went paleo." It was this switch that made me improve dramatically. However, after indulging in salsa and marinara a few too many times, I was right back to flaring up again. I started reading about nightshades (a variety of plants and vegetables including tomatoes, white potatoes, and peppers) and came across the Autoimmune Protocol. I decided to give it a try. But within two weeks I quit, tired of the ever-increasing restrictions. Shortly afterward, however, I regretted the decision and decided to give it another shot. This time I resolved to figure out how to cook and bake safe foods that tasted amazing.

A few months in, my symptoms had vanished. I rarely even felt like I had an autoimmune disease. I began learning to listen to my body like never before; I learned that although I love starches, my body likes to keep them limited, so I reduced my starches to little bites and occasional small treats. I learned that even a common cold could trigger symptoms, so I didn't get anxious if a few symptoms popped in for a spell. I learned that even though I was ready to start making reintroductions into my diet after one month (and four months, and six months...), my body wasn't there yet. I also learned that cheating on my diet was never worth it. Can I emphasize that once more? *Cheating is never worth the potential symptoms or flare-ups.* Until the gut has healed enough to make successful reintroductions, I have found it is best to eat strictly within the elimination diet. Most of all, though, I learned to cook and bake in a whole new way.

I hope you fall in love with these meals and treats just as I did, and that these recipes help bridge the gap between a standard diet and the paleo Autoimmune Protocol. This diet can help you, and you can do it!

Here's to health, happiness, and really good food!

Bre'anna Emmitt

What is an autoimmune disease?

In most people, bodies trigger an inflammatory response to combat illnesses like the common cold and the flu. However, in people with autoimmune diseases, these responses are in overdrive. Rather than just attacking germs and viruses, these faulty immune systems attack healthy body tissue as well. Depending on how a particular body is wired, the immune system can attack the brain or spinal cord (multiple sclerosis), the joints (rheumatoid arthritis), the intestines (celiac, colitis, and Crohn's disease), the spine (ankylosing spondylitis), the thyroid (Hashimoto's or Graves' disease), the skin (psoriasis and lichen planus), major organs (lupus erythematosus), or any other part of the body via hundreds of varying autoimmune diseases or immune-related disorders (like allergies and eczema).

Why paleo?

The paleo diet has been gaining a lot of popularity over the last few years and for good reason. The paleo diet avoids factory-produced, synthetic, and unhealthy foods and replaces them with the foods our bodies were designed to eat: fruits, vegetables, seafood, and meats.

When people begin to eat this way, they often notice drastic changes in the way they feel. Suddenly little bodily quirks and annoyances are gone, their energy skyrockets, they adjust to a healthy weight, and their moods are better. And for people with autoimmune diseases, their symptoms begin to fade away. Scientist and researcher, Sarah Ballantyne, PhD, wrote a book called *The Paleo Approach* to explain the science behind this phenomenon. She also offers a thorough elimination diet to help people figure out exactly which foods trigger their particular symptoms (more on that a little later). The recipes in this cookbook are based on that elimination diet. Unlike the standard paleo diet, this elimination diet is not only free of grains, dairy, soy, beans, and legumes, but also free of nightshades (tomatoes, white potatoes, and peppers), nuts, seeds, and eggs. Switching to a paleo diet can be extremely difficult. That's exactly why I wrote this cookbook—to help people make this transition seamlessly, healthfully, and deliciously!

Getting your family on board

If you have a spouse or children, you already know the daunting task of getting everyone to eat the same meal – let alone enjoy it. I recommend taking this process thoughtfully with each individual. For you, you may have a spouse who has been begging you to eat more healthfully, so they will jump right on board. I knew my husband was raised on bread and pasta, so making a dramatic switch would have sent him into a food rebellion of takeout meals (I mean this in the most loving way, Chris!). You might have similar issues with your loved ones. For this reason, I decided to take things slowly and, like I've already discussed, keep my ingredient lists secret until I knew he was enjoying the food. For example, when I started making Nomato Sauce – a tomato-free marinara sauce (page 114), I didn't tell him it wasn't tomato-based because I knew he hated beets (for the record, he didn't notice the difference and ate a second helping). I also didn't force zucchini noodles or spaghetti squash on him for pasta right away. For me, the non-negotiable was keeping gluten out of the house, so I made an organic corn/rice blend of gluten-free pasta for him, and I ate the spaghetti squash with my dinner. I am not one to cook two meals to make everyone happy, but taking one extra step to ensure everyone enjoys a nourishing meal is fine with me – especially since the other members of my family do not appear to have major sensitivities other than to gluten and soy.

More than anything, however, following trusted recipes and making delicious food is the most guaranteed way to make sure your family will enjoy eating healthy and nourishing meals! I'll always believe if food tastes great, people will eat it.

Paleo versus the Autoimmune Protocol: What to eat and what to avoid

I am often asked the difference between a paleo diet and the Autoimmune Protocol. In short, the Autoimmune Protocol follows a paleo diet with additional restrictions and is meant to reduce or eliminate symptoms and progression of autoimmune diseases.

The Autoimmune Protocol is not meant to be a permanent diet, but a temporary elimination diet. The goal is to eliminate all potential immune-triggering foods, and reintroduce them – one at a time – to help determine true food sensitivities. The rule is simple: if you reintroduce a food and have a reaction or return of symptoms, it's best to eliminate that food either permanently or until you are able to successfully reintroduce it into your diet (more on this in a bit). This cookbook contains recipes that are 100% compliant with the elimination phase of the Autoimmune Protocol.

Suggested Reading for more information and the science behind the Autoimmune Protocol: *The Paleo Approach* by Sarah Ballantyne, PhD.

Paleo Foods to Eat:	Autoimmune Protocol Foods to Eat:
fish	fish
meat	meat
all vegetables and fruits	vegetables, excluding nightshades
nuts	fruits
seeds	healthy fats and oils
eggs	
healthy fats and oils	

Foods to Avoid:	Foods to Eliminate:
grains	grains
legumes	legumes
soy	soy
refined sugars	refined sugars
dairy	dairy
refined, processed foods	refined, processed foods
processed oils	processed oils
	nightshades
	eggs
	nuts (including nut oils and butters)
	seeds (including seed-based oils, butters, and spices)
	berry-based spices (i.e. black pepper)
	cocoa
	alcohol
	coffee

Reintroductions

For those with autoimmune diseases, food reintroductions should take place after the immune system has significantly calmed and symptoms have vanished or greatly reduced. For some, this may be after one month, for others it may be more than a year. Much to my initial dismay, I seem to be part of the latter category.

Reintroductions should be made cautiously, attentively, and slowly – with only one reintroduction every 3 to 7 days. If you notice odd or returning symptoms, feel fatigued or bloated, it's best to eliminate that food again and retry in a few months. If the reaction is severe, the food may need to be eliminated long term or permanently. Reintroductions are typically best made in the following four-stage approach, although which food you try first in each category is completely up to your preference!

Reintroduction Table[1]

Stage 1	Stage 3
egg yolks	pistachios and cashews
berry-based spices (i.e. black pepper)	coffee
seed-based spices (i.e. cumin)	grass-fed cream and fermented dairy (i.e. yogurt)
podded legumes (i.e. green beans and snow peas)	mild nightshades (i.e. paprika, eggplant and sweet peppers)
seed and nut oils (i.e. sesame oil)	
grass-fed ghee (clarified butter)	
Stage 2	**Stage 4**
egg whites	other grass-fed dairy products
cocoa	other nightshades (i.e. white potatoes, chili peppers, and tomatoes)
grass-fed butter	other legumes
seeds and nuts (except pistachios and cashews)	white rice and other gluten-free grains
alcohol in small amounts	alcohol in moderate amounts

[1]Sarah Ballantyne, PhD, *The Paleo Approach: Reverse Autoimmune Disease and Heal Your Body* (Las Vegas: Victory Belt Publishing, Inc. 2013), 334. Reprinted with permission from The Paleo Approach by Sarah Ballantyne, PhD.

Important Baking Tip

Measure precisely and follow the recipes. If you're like me, you don't do this naturally. I learned quickly, however, that grain-free baking is not nearly as forgiving as wheat-based baking. The wet-to-dry ratio needs to be just right in order for the final product to reach perfection.

The ingredients and stocking your pantry

If this is your first time opening a paleo cookbook, you're probably thinking, *What are these weird ingredients?* Don't worry, I thought the same thing.

In order to bake and cook successfully on a paleo or AIP diet, a lot of new ingredients must be added to your pantry. You can take one of two approaches: Get rid of all your non-paleo foods and stock up on paleo pantry staples, or gradually switch over as recipes and ingredient lists call. I took the latter approach, and it worked well for me (although I rid my house of all gluten immediately following my Celiac diagnosis).

AIP Ingredient:	Description:	Where to find it:	Paleo Substitution:
arrowroot flour (also called arrowroot starch)	Arrowroot flour is a very fine, powdery starch used for baking and thickening. I often use arrowroot in combination with coconut flour in baking to help give a lighter, airier texture. It also replaces cornstarch in thickening sauces.	• health food stores • Amazon	Arrowroot flour is a common flour replacement in both paleo and AIP diets. Tapioca starch, which is also AIP compliant, can often be substituted for arrowroot flour in a 1:1 ratio, although results are not guaranteed.
avocado oil	Avocado oil is a healthy oil with a very mild taste and high-heat stability. I always keep this on hand and use it in place of vegetable oil or olive oil in many of my recipes. Olive oil is AIP but is not as high-heat stable.	• major grocers • health food stores • Amazon I have found that bulk grocery warehouses typically have the best prices.	Avocado oil is a common oil used in both paleo and AIP diets.
carob	Carob is a cocoa powder substitute.	• major grocers • health food stores • Amazon	Cocoa and carob can be substituted at a 1:1 ratio. (Note: Cocoa is a Stage 2 AIP reintroduction)
coconut aminos	Coconut aminos are a great substitute for soy sauce in Asian dishes.	• major grocers • health food stores • Amazon	Coconut aminos are a common soy sauce replacement in both paleo and AIP diets.
coconut butter (also called coconut manna or creamed coconut)	Coconut butter is ground coconut. (Just as peanut butter is ground peanuts, coconut butter is ground coconut.)	• major grocers • health food stores • Amazon Coconut butter is usually found by the nut butters.	I have found some baking recipes can evenly substitute almond butter for coconut butter, although it is not always a guaranteed result. (Note: Almond butter is a Stage 2 AIP reintroduction)
coconut cream	Coconut cream replaces heavy cream.	• Asian grocery markets • Amazon Coconut cream can be scooped off of the top of a refrigerated can of coconut milk (the cream separates from the water at cold temperatures), or bought in cartons. For a carton, I recommend the brand Aroy-D, in which the only ingredient is coconut cream. Aroy-D can be found on Amazon or in Asian grocery markets.	Coconut cream is a common dairy replacement in both paleo and AIP diets.

AIP Ingredient:	Description:	Where to find it:	Paleo Substitution:
coconut flour	Coconut flour replaces other baking flours, but due to its high absorbency, it does not substitute well at a 1:1 ratio. My favorite brand is Bob's Red Mill because it is very finely ground and does not require sifting.	• major grocers • health food stores • Amazon	Coconut flour is used in paleo and AIP diets.
coconut milk (canned or in a shelf-stable carton, not refrigerated)	Coconut milk replaces other milks. When refrigerated, the coconut cream separates from the coconut water and rises to the top from the coconut water.	• major grocers • health food stores • Amazon Look for varieties with no added gums or carrageenan. The only ingredients should be coconut milk and water.	Coconut milk is used in Paleo and AIP diets. Nut milks like almond milk can usually be substituted in baked goods, but items like ice cream will not be as creamy with almond milk. (Note: Almond milk is a Stage 2 AIP reintroduction.)
coconut oil	Coconut oil is a healthy cooking oil that is solid below 76 degrees (F) or 24 degrees (C) and liquid when above those temperatures Since it carries a mild coconut flavor, I typically reserve coconut oil for sweeter dishes.	• major grocers • health food stores • Amazon I have found that bulk grocery warehouses typically have the best prices.	Coconut oil is a common oil used in both paleo and AIP diets.
collagen	Collagen is a powder I use in smoothies for added protein. It is tasteless and without texture, and it is also full of healthy amino acids. It is beneficial for promoting healthy skin, hair, nails, bones and joints. I recommend Great Lakes brand. Their collagen is in a green can.	• Amazon	Collagen is a healthy supplement used in both paleo and AIP diets.
evaporated cane juice	Evaporated cane juice is a granular (not liquid) sweetener, similar in appearance to refined sugar, although the coloring is a bit darker. Evaporated cane juice has the same glycemic index as maple syrup and carries the vitamins and minerals that are lost in the refining process of white table sugar.	• major grocers • health food stores • Amazon	This granular sugar is not easily substituted with liquid paleo sweeteners like honey or maple syrup. Evaporated cane juice is used in both paleo and AIP diets in moderation.
fish sauce	Fish sauce is a salty liquid condiment similar to Worcestershire sauce. Warning: A little goes a long way.	• major grocers • health food stores • Amazon	Fish sauce is a condiment used in both paleo and AIP diets.
gelatin	Gelatin is a powder similar to collagen, except gelatin solidifies when mixed with liquid. I use this often as a "Gelatin Egg Substitute" (page 18), and I keep a can or two on hand at all times. Gelatin has the same health benefits as collagen and binds egg-free baked goods beautifully. I recommend Great Lakes brand. Their gelatin is in an orange-red can.	• Amazon	In baked goods, eggs can be substituted for gelatin. The general rule is that one egg can be substituted for one Gelatin Egg Substitute (page 18). Do not substitute eggs for gelatin in unbaked goods (i.e. Key Lime Pie on page 128) (Note: Whole eggs are a Stage 2 AIP reintroduction.)

AIP Ingredient:	Description:	Where to find it:	Paleo Substitution:
mace	Mace is a spice from the same plant and with similar taste as nutmeg, but it is not made from the seed, so it is considered safe for the Autoimmune Protocol.	• major grocers • health food stores • Amazon	Nutmeg can be substituted for mace at a 4:1 ratio. If the recipe calls for 1/4 teaspoon of mace, use 1 teaspoon of nutmeg. (Note: Nutmeg is a seed-based spice and is a Stage 1 AIP reintroduction.)
maple syrup (100% pure)	Maple syrup is a liquid sweetener used in many paleo and AIP recipes. This is not the maple-flavored syrup made by many breakfast syrup companies, but 100% pure maple syrup.	• major grocers • health food stores • Amazon I have found that bulk grocery warehouses typically have the best prices.	Maple syrup is a common sweetener used in both paleo and AIP diets.
nutritional yeast	Nutritional yeast is a flaky, deactivated yeast and has a strong cheesy flavor. It is used in paleo recipes to replicate a cheesy taste in dishes.	• health food stores • Amazon	Nutritional yeast has a cheese flavor used in both paleo and AIP diets. Cheese and dairy products are not considered paleo, but they are a Stage 4 reintroduction on the AIP diet. If you are able to reintroduce cheese, you may use your favorite cheeses in place of nutritional yeast. You will need to add much more cheese than the amount of nutritional yeast called for in the recipe since nutritional yeast is very potent and only a small amount is used.
palm shortening	Palm shortening is a healthy, non-hydrogenated white shortening. It's appearance and use are similar to a typical baking shortening	• major grocers • health food stores • Amazon	Palm shortening is not easily substituted in many recipes. Coconut oil may work in some recipes, but the results are not guaranteed.
raw honey	Raw honey is a liquid sweetener used in many paleo and AIP recipes. Raw honey is honey that has not been heated or filtered, leaving it as natural and nutritious as possible. Locally sourced is best.	• major grocers • health food stores • Amazon	Raw honey is a common sweetener used in both paleo and AIP diets.
sea salt	Sea salt is used instead of table salt in paleo diets. Refined table salt has been stripped of nearly all of its natural minerals, whereas sea salt is unrefined and retains its many healthy, valuable and vital minerals.	• major grocers • health food stores • Amazon	Various colors of sea salt (pink, etc.) can be used in the recipes in this book.
vanilla extract (100% pure)	Pure vanilla extract (not imitation) is used in paleo and AIP recipes. In AIP recipes, it is cooked or baked to burn off the alcohol. Since alcohol is a Stage 2 AIP reintroduction, burning off the alcohol is not necessary if it has been successfully reintroduced.	• major grocers • health food stores • Amazon • bulk grocery warehouses	Vanilla extract is used in both paleo and AIP diets.

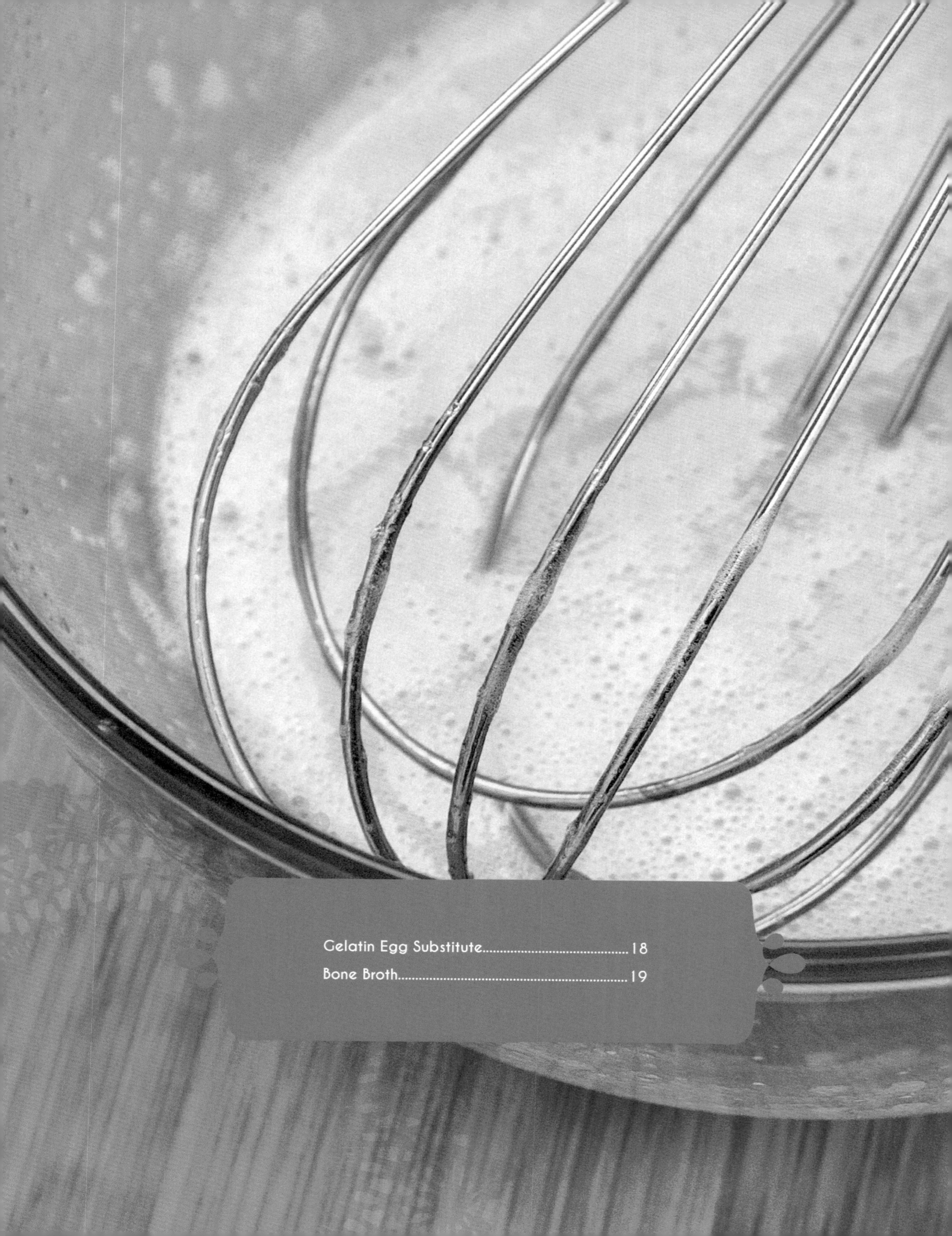

BASICS

Gelatin Egg Substitute

While eggs are a nutritious part of a standard diet as well as a paleo diet, they are not part of the elimination stage of the Autoimmune Protocol because they can stimulate an immune response. This substitute does not create rise in baked goods like a real egg does, but it binds beautifully.

🍴 Prep Time: 5 minutes   🎁 Yield: substitute for 1 egg

Ingredients:

1 tablespoon grass-fed gelatin

1 tablespoon lukewarm water

2 tablespoons boiling or very hot water

Directions:

1 Whisk the gelatin into lukewarm water. The mixture will create a rubbery gel.

2 Add the boiling water and whisk vigorously until completely dissolved and frothy. Use immediately; if it sits too long, it will solidify and be unusable.

Tips:

Once eggs are successfully introduced into the diet, feel free to substitute one egg for each "gelatin egg substitute" called for throughout this book, with the exception of unbaked goods, which require the use of gelatin to solidify properly (i.e. the filling from the Key Lime Pie on page 128).

Bone Broth

This broth recipe is as simple as they come. Personally, I prefer a neutral broth, so I prepare mine unseasoned and without any herbs or vegetables in my stock.

🍴 Prep Time: 5 minutes   ⏰ Cooking Time: 12 hours

🎁 Yield: 2 quarts broth

Ingredients:

2 1/2	pounds boney chicken or beef parts
1 1/2	tablespoons apple cider vinegar
1	teaspoon sea salt
3-4	quarts water

Directions:

1.   Place bones, vinegar, and salt in a slow cooker. Cover the bones with water, making sure there is at least 1/2 inch of room under the lid. Cover and simmer on low for 12 hours.

2.   When finished cooking, strain the broth through a wire mesh colander or cheesecloth, skimming the fat off the top. Store for a few days in the refrigerator or freeze for storage up to 6 months.

Appetizers

Grape Bruschetta

This bruschetta is savory, sweet, and absolutely to die for! It pairs perfectly with Wheatless Thins (page 30) or Flatbread (page 50).

🍴 Prep Time: 10 minutes   🎁 Yield: 2 cups

Ingredients:

2	cups chopped red grapes
1/2	cup coarsely chopped fresh basil (about 20 leaves)
2	cloves garlic, minced
1	tablespoon olive oil
1	tablespoon Balsamic vinegar
1/2	teaspoon sea salt

Directions:

Stir all the ingredients together. Serve with flatbread (p. 50) or Wheatless Thins (p. 30).

Stuffed Mushrooms

These little mushrooms are an absolutely scrumptious and savory starter! I love to serve these for a dinner party, or enjoy them as a side to White Lasagna with Turkey and Zucchini (page 96) or zucchini noodles with Nomato Sauce (page 114).

🍴 Prep Time: 15 minutes	⏰ Cooking Time: 30 minutes	🎁 Yield: 6 servings

Ingredients:

1   pound baby bella or button mushrooms

2   tablespoons chopped fresh chives, plus 1 tablespoon for garnish

2   tablespoons coconut flour

2   tablespoons avocado oil

1   tablespoon nutritional yeast

1   tablespoon coconut aminos, plus more for sprinkling

1/4 teaspoon salt

1/4 teaspoon garlic powder

Directions:

1   Preheat the oven to 350°F and line a baking sheet with parchment paper.

2   Separate the mushroom stems from the caps. Place the stems in a blender and arrange the caps on a parchment-lined baking sheet.

3   Add the remaining ingredients to the blender; process until smooth.

4   Spoon the filling into the mushroom caps just until level with the top. Sprinkle with additional coconut aminos and remaining tablespoon of chives.

5   Bake for 30 minutes.

Nightshade–Free Red Salsa

Salsa has always been a staple in our house, so eliminating nightshades really threw a kink in our Mexican food habits. This quick and easy salsa is a great impostor and makes me forget I can't eat the real stuff.

Prep Time: 5 minutes   Yield: 2 cups

Ingredients:

1/3   cup diced canned beets, drained and rinsed
       thoroughly

1   (14.5-ounce) can carrots, drained and rinsed

1/2   bunch cilantro

1   small white onion, quartered

1/4   cup lime juice

2   cloves garlic, peeled

3/4   teaspoon sea salt

Directions:

Place all the ingredients in a blender or food processor and blend until uniform in consistency.

Mexican Green Sauce

Everyone who tries it loves this green sauce! This absolutely crave-worthy sauce is a refreshing cross between a creamy guacamole and a green salsa.

🍴 Prep Time: 5 minutes   🎁 Yield: 2 cups

Ingredients:

1/2	large cucumber, peeled and cut into chunks
1	medium white onion, cut into chunks
1/2	bunch cilantro
3	tablespoons lime juice
1	large avocado, pit and skin removed
1	clove garlic, peeled
1/2	teaspoon sea salt

Directions:

Place all the ingredients in a blender or food processor and blend until creamy.

Queso

This "queso" recipe is a cheesy and creamy replacement when you have a cheese craving. It's perfect as a dip for Plantain Chips (page 27) or tortilla chips, or for drizzling on your favorite tacos.

🍴 Prep Time: 10 minutes   ⏰ Cooking Time: 20 minutes

🎁 Yield: 3 cups

Ingredients:

4	cups fresh or frozen cauliflower, cut into florets
1/2	cup chopped carrots
1	cup Bone Broth (Page 19) or water
3	tablespoons olive oil
1	tablespoon nutritional yeast
1	teaspoon sea salt
1/4	teaspoon onion powder
1	tablespoon arrowroot flour (optional)

Directions:

1 Bring a large pot of water to a boil. Add the cauliflower and carrots. Boil for 15 minutes until very tender. Meanwhile, place the remaining ingredients in a blender.

2 When the cauliflower and carrots are tender, drain and discard the water. Add the vegetables to the blender. Blend on high until liquefied. Reheat on the stove top before serving, if necessary.

Tips:

If the queso begins to dry out, you can add water or broth and whisk or re-blend.

Plantain Chips

These chips deliver the perfect crunch! Dip them in Nightshade-Free Red Salsa (page 24) or Mexican Green Sauce (page 25).

🍴 Prep Time: 10 minutes	⏰ Cooking Time: 15 minutes	🎁 Yield: 2 cups

Ingredients:

6-8   cups avocado oil or palm shortening

2   green plantains, very thinly sliced

       sea salt

Tips:

Use a paring knife to peel green plantains.

Directions:

1   Heat two inches of oil in a deep pot over medium-high heat until a small drop of water sizzles when it hits the oil.

2   In small batches, add the plantains to the hot oil and cook for about 1 minute or until the edges of the chips start to turn golden brown.

3   Line a pan with paper towels. Remove chips with a slotted spoon and transfer to the lined pan. Sprinkle immediately with salt to taste. Cool and serve.

Wings with Wasabi Ranch Dipping Sauce

Fall-off-the-bone tender, gorgeously colored, and with a good amount of heat in the dressing, these wings are the perfect party pleaser. Serve alongside carrots and celery for the full wings experience!

Prep Time: 20 minutes   Cooking Time: 8 hours   Yield: 3 pounds

Ingredients:

For the wings:

3   pounds chicken wings or drumettes, rinsed and patted dry

2   large carrots, cut into 2-inch chunks

1/2 cup Bone Broth (page 19)

3   tablespoons honey

4   cloves garlic, minced

1   teaspoon onion powder

1/2 teaspoon sea salt

For the dipping sauce:

2/3 cup avocado oil

2   tablespoons palm shortening

2   teaspoons apple cider vinegar

2   teaspoons wasabi powder

1-3 inches horseradish root, peeled and chopped (depending on your preferred spice level)

1/2 teaspoon garlic powder

1/2 teaspoon sea salt

1/4 teaspoon onion powder

1   teaspoon dried parsley

1   teaspoon dried chives

1/2 teaspoon dried dill

Directions:

1   Place the wings and carrots in a slow cooker.

2   In a small mixing bowl, whisk together the broth, honey, garlic, onion powder, and salt. Pour the mixture over chicken and carrots. Cook on low for 8 hours.

3   To prepare the sauce, in a blender, blend the avocado oil, palm shortening, vinegar, wasabi powder, horseradish, garlic powder, salt, and onion powder until smooth and creamy. Add the parsley, chives, and dill. Pulse until combined. Refrigerate until ready to serve.

4   Line a baking sheet with aluminum foil. With tongs, carefully remove the wings and arrange them 1 inch apart on the baking sheet.

5   Pour the liquid and carrots from the slow cooker into a blender. Blend until liquefied. Brush the blended mixture liberally onto the wings.

6   Place the wings under a broiler. Set the broiler to high and broil for 4 to 6 minutes, watching carefully. The wings are ready when bubbly and crispy. Serve hot with the dipping sauce on the side.

Wheatless Thins

I'm almost positive my husband could survive on snack foods alone. For him, "just a few bites" inevitably turns into an empty box and a full tummy. According to him, these crackers are gorge-worthy! Top them with a bit of Spinach and Artichoke Dip (Page 31) to turn them into a delightful appetizer!

Prep Time: 10 minutes　　　Cooking Time: 35 minutes　　　Yield: 30 crackers

Ingredients:

2　　large green plantains

1/3　cup Bone Broth (page 19) or water

1/3　cup avocado oil

1/4　teaspoon sea salt for blender ingredients, plus

　　　additional 1/4 teaspoon for sprinkling

Tips:

Use a paring knife to peel green plantains.

Directions:

1　Preheat the oven to 325°F and fully line the bottom of a large baking sheet or 12x18-inch jelly roll pan with parchment paper.

2　To a blender, add the plantains, bone broth, avocado oil, and 1/4 teaspoon sea salt. Blend until smooth. Pour the mixture onto the parchment-lined baking sheet and, with a rubber spatula, spread it thinly all the way to the sides of the pan.

3　Sprinkle with the remaining 1/4 teaspoon of sea salt. Bake for 15 minutes. Remove the pan and score with a pizza cutter into desired cracker sizes. Return to the oven and bake for 20-30 more minutes, until perfectly crunchy and not bendable.

Spinach and Artichoke Dip

A creamy replacement for its dairy- and gluten-laden sibling, this dip is certain to please paleo and non-paleo diners alike! I love to keep these ingredients on hand for a quick appetizer when friends pop in to visit. Pair this dip with Flatbread (page 50), Wheatless Thins (page 30) or fresh carrots and celery for a veggie treat!

🍴 Prep Time: 10 minutes   ⏰ Cooking Time: 30 minutes   🎁 Yield: 8 servings

Ingredients:

1   (8-ounce) package frozen chopped spinach

3/4   cup avocado oil

2   (14-ounce) cans quartered artichoke hearts, drained well

3   cloves garlic, peeled

1   teaspoon sea salt

Tip:

This dish can be served as a cold dip, too! Instead of baking it, simply serve the dip after combining all of the ingredients or cover and chill in the refrigerator.

Directions:

1   Preheat the oven to 375°F.

2   Over medium heat, bring 1/4 cup water to a boil in a medium saucepan. Add the spinach to the boiling water. Return to a boil and boil for 6-8 minutes, until hot and bubbly throughout. Drain the water from the spinach, carefully pressing with a large spoon to squeeze out as much excess water as possible. Set aside.

3   Add the avocado oil, one can of artichokes, garlic and salt to a food processor or blender. Process until very creamy, similar to the consistency of ricotta cheese.

4   Add the spinach and remaining can of artichokes to the processor. Pulse to combine and chop the additional artichoke hearts. Spread the mixture into an 8 by 8-inch casserole dish or 9-inch pie plate. Bake for 25-30 minutes until hot and bubbly throughout.

Condiments, Dressings, & Seasonings

Dairy-Free Butter

There simply is nothing like salty butter on baked sweet potatoes or Banana Bread Bars (page 44). This is a quick and easy substitute to give that creamy, salty, and buttery flavor that's easily missed on a dairy-free diet.

Prep time: 5 minutes   Yield: 1/2 cup

Ingredients:

1/3	cup plus 1 tablespoon palm shortening
2	tablespoons olive oil
1/4	teaspoon sea salt

Directions:

Place all the ingredients in a medium mixing bowl. Beat on low until combined and creamy. Store in a small, covered dish at room temperature (for soft butter) or in the refrigerator (for solid butter).

Creamy Egg-Free Mayo

Mayo adds moisture to a dry sandwich and can transform a boring salad into a crisp and creamy meal. This mayo is a flash to make and keeps beautifully for long periods of time.

Prep Time: 10 minutes　　　　　　　　　**Yield:** 1 cup

Ingredients:

2/3　cup avocado oil

1/3　cup palm shortening

2　　teaspoons lemon juice

1/2　teaspoon sea salt

Directions:

1　Place all the ingredients in a blender or small mixing bowl. Blend or beat on high until whipped and creamy (about 4-5 minutes with a hand mixer).

2　Store in the refrigerator. Mixture will thicken and firm up, but will still spread easily.

Tips:

For a cream-colored mayo as photographed, replace 1 tablespoon of the avocado oil with olive oil.

If the mayo does not whip properly, refrigerating the mixture should still firm it up nicely.

Variations:

Aioli: Add 1/2 teaspoon garlic powder to the recipe before mixing.

Dill Aioli: Add 1/2 teaspoon each garlic powder and dried dill weed before mixing. If using a blender, pulse in the dill after the mayo and garlic is whipped.

Condiments, Dressings, & Seasonings

No-Nightshade Ketchup

My kids love this ketchup, and my husband has never asked if it's "real ketchup"—which is always a sign that a recipe is a keeper!

🍴 Prep Time: 10 minutes   ⏰ Cooking Time: 45 minutes

👥 Yield: 1 1/2 cups

Ingredients:

2/3	cup peeled and chopped red beets
1	cup peeled and chopped carrots
1/2	cup chopped yellow onion
2/3	cup water
1/2	cup apple cider vinegar
1/2	cup honey
1	teaspoon sea salt
1/4	teaspoon ground cloves

Directions:

1   Fill a medium saucepan halfway with water and bring it to a boil. Add the beets, carrots, and onion. Boil for 10 to 15 minutes until tender.

2   While the vegetables are cooking, add the remaining ingredients to the blender and set aside.

3   When the vegetables are tender, drain them and add them to the blender as well. Blend on high until liquefied.

4   Transfer the blended vegetable mixture to a medium sauce pan. Cover and bring the mixture to a boil over medium-high heat. Uncover and reduce heat to low. Simmer for 30 to 40 minutes, until the sauce is thickened and reduced by half. Remove from heat and cool completely. Store in the refrigerator for up to a week or in the freezer for up to six months.

Barbecue Sauce

If you miss a tomato-based barbecue sauce, this recipe is for you! It's perfect on burgers, ribs, or anything grilled!

🍴 Prep Time: 15 minutes   ⏰ Cooking Time: 45 minutes   🎁 Yield: 1 1/2 cups

---

Ingredients:

1/2	cup peeled and chopped red beets
1/2	cup peeled and chopped carrots
5	cloves garlic, peeled and halved
1/3	cup water
1/2	cup honey or maple syrup
3	tablespoons apple cider vinegar
2	teaspoons smoked sea salt
2	teaspoons capers
1	teaspoon fish sauce
1 1/2	teaspoons onion powder

Directions:

1 Fill a medium saucepan halfway with water and bring it to a boil. Add the beets, carrots, and garlic. Boil for 10 to 15 minutes until tender.

2 While the vegetables are cooking, add the remaining ingredients to the blender and set aside.

3 When the vegetables are tender, drain them and add them to the blender as well. Blend on high until liquefied.

4 Transfer the blended vegetable mixture to the medium sauce pan. Cover and bring to a boil, then uncover and cook on low for 35 minutes until thickened and reduced considerably. Cool completely and store in the refrigerator for up to a week or in the freezer for up to six months.

Peach Barbecue Sauce

This just may be my favorite barbecue sauce in the world. Tangy and sweet, it is the perfect complement to shrimp, grilled chicken, or pork chops. It freezes well, too, so make a big batch and freeze it in individual portions!

🍴 Prep Time: 10 minutes   ⏰ Cooking Time: 40 minutes

🎁 Yield: 1 1/2 cups

Ingredients:

2   tablespoons coconut oil

1   medium yellow onion, chopped coarsely

4   cloves garlic, minced

1   teaspoon smoked sea salt

1   (12-ounce) package frozen peaches (about 3 cups)

2   tablespoons apple cider vinegar

1/3   cup honey

1   tablespoon chopped, fresh oregano or 1 teaspoon
        dried oregano

Directions:

1   Heat the oil over medium heat in a large saucepan. Add
        the onion, garlic, and salt. Cook for 5 to 7 minutes
        until tender.

2   Add all the remaining ingredients except for the oregano
        and stir to combine. Heat the mixture over high heat until
        the liquids begin to boil. Decrease the heat to low or
        medium-low, keeping the sauce simmering. Cook uncovered
        for 30 minutes, until the mixture is reduced by one-third
        and thickened.

3   Transfer the mixture to a blender and blend on high until
        smooth. Return the mixture to the saucepan, add the
        oregano, and simmer on low for 5 to 10 more minutes
        until thick and glossy. Cool completely and store in the
        refrigerator for up to a week or in the freezer for up to
        six months.

Ranch Dressing

I've always loved salads, but I tired of them rather quickly once I went AIP. It wasn't the actual salads I was tired of, but rather the same boring mixture of oil and vinegar. This recipe came out of a craving for some creamy ranch-style dressing to liven up my greens, and it quickly became a staple. It also keeps well for long periods of time in the refrigerator, so don't be afraid to double or triple the batch!

Prep Time: 7 minutes   Yield: 1 cup

Ingredients:

2/3	cup avocado oil
2	tablespoons palm shortening
2	teaspoons apple cider vinegar
1	teaspoon dried parsley
1	teaspoon dried chives
1/2	teaspoon dried dill
1/2	teaspoon garlic powder
1/2	teaspoon sea salt
1/4	teaspoon onion powder

Directions:

In a medium mixing bowl, combine all ingredients and mix until combined and creamy. Store in the refrigerator, shaking or stirring if necessary to recombine.

Seed–Free Mustard

A great alternative to mustard, this seed-free version has the same vinegar tang and a hint of spice. When stored in the refrigerator it will harden. Simply let it come to room temperature before serving.

🍴 Prep Time: 5 minutes   🎁 Yield: 1/3 cup

Ingredients:

3   tablespoons coconut butter, softened

1   tablespoon water

2   tablespoons apple cider vinegar

3/4 teaspoon ground turmeric

1/2 teaspoon sea salt

1/4 teaspoon garlic powder

Directions:

In a medium mixing bowl, combine all the ingredients together until creamy. Store in the refrigerator and let soften at room temperature before using.

Seasonings

Barbecue

🍴 Prep Time: 5 minutes
👥 Yield: 1 cup

Ingredients:

1/3 cup evaporated cane juice
1/4 cup smoked sea salt
2 tablespoons dried oregano
2 tablespoons garlic powder
2 tablespoons onion powder
1 teaspoon ground turmeric
1/2 teaspoon ground mace

House

🍴 Prep Time: 5 minutes
👥 Yield: 2/3 cup

Ingredients:

1/4 cup sea salt
1/4 cup dried parsley
2 tablespoons dried minced garlic
2 tablespoons onion powder

Italian

🍴 Prep Time: 5 minutes
👥 Yield: 1 cup

Ingredients:

1/4 cup oregano
1/4 cup sea salt
2 tablespoons garlic powder
2 tablespoons onion powder
2 tablespoons dried parsley
2 tablespoons dried basil
1 teaspoon dried thyme

Directions:

Place all the ingredients of the selected seasoning in a jar or container. Shake to combine. Store sealed at room temperature in a dry location. To use, rub or sprinkle onto meat or desired food, and cook or grill as desired.

Breads
& Muffins

Banana Bread Bars

Since this is egg-free banana bread, it won't rise like a traditional loaf. But don't worry! You'll get the same great texture by baking it in a 9 by 13-inch pan. And honestly, don't we all cut our "loaves" into slices anyway?

Prep Time: 15 minutes　　　Cooking Time: 25 minutes　　　Yield: 16 bars

Ingredients:

1	cup mashed ripe bananas
1/4	cup coconut oil, plus additional for greasing the pan
1/2	cup coconut butter, softened
1	tablespoon honey
1	teaspoon vanilla extract
1 1/2	teaspoon lemon juice
1/4	cup coconut flour
1/2	cup arrowroot flour
1/2	teaspoon sea salt
1/2	teaspoon baking soda
1/2	teaspoon ground cinnamon

Directions:

1. Preheat the oven to 350°F. Lightly grease a 9 by 13-inch pan with coconut oil.

2. In a large mixing bowl or stand mixer, add the bananas, oil, coconut butter, honey, vanilla, and lemon juice. Mix on medium until smooth.

3. In a small mixing bowl, whisk together the flours, salt, baking soda, and cinnamon.

4. Pour the dry ingredients into the wet ingredients and mix until combined. Spread the batter into the pan.

5. Bake for 24 to 27 minutes until a toothpick inserted into the center comes out clean and the edges pull away from the sides of the pan. Cut into 2 by 3-inch) bars.

Tip:

If your bread tastes chewy out of the oven, don't fret! The texture will firm up as it rests. You can accomplish this by refrigerating it for a bit to firm it up or letting it sit overnight. At cool temperatures, the bread will firm up significantly because of the coconut butter. Store at room temperature for true banana bread texture.

Pumpkin Bread Bars

These pumpkin bread bars are velvety, mildly sweet, and have the perfect amount of spice. They're also ideal for those who adhere to a starch-free or fruit-sweetened diet. Like most coconut flour recipes, I find these improve with time!

🍴 Prep Time: 15 minutes   ⏰ Cooking Time: 25 minutes

🎁 Yield: 18 bars

Ingredients:

1/3	cup coconut flour
1	teaspoon baking soda
1/2	teaspoon sea salt
2	teaspoons ground cinnamon
1/2	teaspoon ground ginger
1/4	teaspoon ground cloves
1/8	teaspoon ground mace
3/4	cup pumpkin puree
1/4	cup coconut oil, plus additional for greasing the pan
1/4	cup coconut butter, softened
1	cup dates, gently packed
1	teaspoon vanilla extract
1 1/2	teaspoon lemon juice
1	Gelatin Egg Substitute (page 18), prepared when directed

Directions:

1. Preheat the oven to 350°F and lightly grease a 9 by 13-inch pan with coconut oil.

2. In a small mixing bowl, whisk together the flour, baking soda, salt, cinnamon, ginger, cloves, and mace.

3. In a food processor, process the pumpkin, oil, coconut butter, dates, vanilla, and lemon juice until smooth.

4. Prepare the gelatin egg. Add it to the food processor and process until combined.

5. Combine the dry ingredients with the wet ingredients in the food processor. Process until smooth. Spread the batter evenly into the pan.

6. Bake for 24 to 27 minutes, until a toothpick inserted into the center comes out clean and the edges pull away from the sides of the pan. Cut into 16 (2 by 3-inch) bars.

Banana Blueberry Muffins

An AIP muffin may seem impossible, but this recipe is carefully crafted to create delicious, beautiful muffins with perfectly rounded tops. In fact, this is one of the recipes I'm most proud of, because it was the first round-top AIP muffin I had seen. Your friends and family definitely won't guess this one is paleo!

🍴 Prep Time: 15 minutes   ⏰ Cooking Time: 30 minutes

🎁 Yield: 12 muffins

Ingredients:

2/3	cup coconut flour
1/2	cup arrowroot flour
1 1/2	teaspoons cream of tartar
1	teaspoon baking soda
1/2	teaspoon sea salt
3/4	cup ripe mashed bananas, at room temperature
1/3	cup coconut oil
1/3	cup coconut butter, softened
1/4	cup honey
2	teaspoons lemon juice
1	teaspoon vanilla extract
1	Gelatin Egg Substitute (page 18), prepared when directed
1	cup fresh or frozen blueberries

Directions:

1   Preheat the oven to 350°F and line a 12-cup muffin tin with paper liners.

2   In a small bowl, whisk together the flours, cream of tartar, baking soda, and salt.

3   In a large mixing bowl or stand mixer, cream together the bananas, oil, coconut butter, honey, lemon juice, and vanilla.

4   Prepare the gelatin egg substitute and add it to the wet ingredients. Beat on medium speed to incorporate.

5   Add the dry ingredients to the wet ingredients in the mixing bowl, beating on medium speed until combined. Fold in the blueberries.

6   Divide and roll the dough into twelve equal balls (about 1/4 cup each). Gently place each ball into a muffin cup. Do not push down; the dough will expand to fill the cup as it bakes.

7   Bake for 30 to 35 minutes, until the edges of the muffins are golden brown and a toothpick inserted into the center comes out clean.

Pumpkin Streusel Muffins

A taste of fall, these muffins are the perfect sweet treat for a holiday or special occasion.

Prep Time: 15 minutes   Cooking Time: 35 minutes

Yield: 12 muffins

Ingredients:

For the muffins:

2/3	cup coconut flour
1/2	cup arrowroot flour
1 1/2	teaspoons cream of tartar
1	teaspoon baking soda
1/2	teaspoon sea salt
2	teaspoons ground cinnamon
1/4	teaspoon ground ginger
1/4	teaspoon ground mace
1/4	teaspoon ground cloves
1 1/4	cups pumpkin puree
1/3	cup coconut butter, softened
1/3	cup coconut oil
1/4	cup maple syrup
2	teaspoons lemon juice
1 1/2	teaspoons vanilla extract
1	Gelatin Egg Substitute (page 18), prepared when directed

For the streusel:

1/4	cup shredded unsweetened coconut
2	tablespoons maple syrup
1	tablespoon coconut oil
1/2	teaspoon ground cinnamon

Directions:

1. Preheat the oven to 350°F and line a 12-cup muffin tin with paper liners.

2. In a small bowl, whisk together the flours, cream of tartar, baking soda, salt, cinnamon, ginger, mace, and cloves.

3. In a large mixing bowl or stand mixer, cream together the pumpkin, coconut butter, oil, maple syrup, lemon juice, and vanilla.

4. Prepare the gelatin egg substitute and add it to the wet ingredients already in the mixer bowl. Beat on medium speed to incorporate.

5. Add the dry ingredients to the wet ingredients in the mixing bowl and beat until combined.

6. Divide and roll the dough into twelve equal balls (about 1/4 cup each). Gently place each ball into a muffin cup. Do not push down; the dough will expand to fill the cup as it bakes.

7. Mix all of the streusel ingredients together in a small bowl. Spoon the streusel mixture onto the muffins and gently spread to coat the tops.

8. Bake for 35 minutes until the muffins are set and firm to the touch.

Mini "Cornbread" Muffins

In my family, "soup night" is synonymous with "cornbread night." This became a real problem when I could no longer have corn or bread. This recipe makes adorable little mini cornbread-like muffins, and when topped with some of my dairy-free "butter" and chives, I doubt anyone will question whether there's corn in them.

Prep Time: 15 minutes   Cooking Time: 17 minutes

Yield: 18 mini muffins

Ingredients:

1/3	cup coconut flour
1/3	cup arrowroot flour
1	teaspoon cream of tartar
3/4	teaspoon baking soda
1/4	teaspoon sea salt
1/3	cup unsweetened applesauce, at room temperature
1/4	cup coconut butter, softened
1 1/2	teaspoons lemon juice
2	tablespoons honey
2	tablespoons coconut oil
1	teaspoon vanilla extract
1	Gelatin Egg Substitute (page 18), prepared when directed
1	recipe Dairy-Free Butter (page 34), optional
1	tablespoon chopped fresh chives for garnish, optional

Directions:

1   Preheat the oven to 350°F and line an 18-cup mini muffin tin with paper liners.

2   In a small mixing bowl, whisk together the flours, cream of tartar, baking soda, and salt.

3   In a large mixing bowl or stand mixer, cream together the applesauce, coconut butter, lemon juice, honey, oil, and vanilla.

4   Prepare the gelatin egg substitute and add it to the mixing bowl. Beat on medium speed to combine.

5   Add the dry ingredients to the wet ingredients, beating on medium speed until combined.

6   Using a tablespoon, scoop out the dough and then roll it into balls. Gently place one ball in each cup. Do not push down; the dough will expand to fill the cup as it bakes.

7   Bake for 17 to 18 minutes until the edges of the muffins are golden brown and a toothpick inserted into the center comes out clean.

8   Remove paper-lined muffins from the pan and cool them completely on a wire rack. Top with dairy-free butter and sprinkle chives over the top.

Biscuits

These biscuits are perfect for sandwiches, with a layer of fruit preserves, or with a big bowl of soup!

🍴 Prep Time: 15 minutes   ⏰ Cooking Time: 12 minutes

🎁 Yield: 5 biscuits

Ingredients:

1/3	cup coconut flour
1/3	cup arrowroot flour
1	teaspoon cream of tartar
3/4	teaspoon baking soda
1/2	teaspoon salt
3	tablespoons water
3	tablespoons avocado oil
1 1/2	teaspoons lemon juice
1	Gelatin Egg Substitute (page 18), prepared when directed

Directions:

1   Preheat the oven to 350°F and line a baking sheet with parchment paper.

2   In a small mixing bowl, combine the flours, cream of tartar, baking soda, and salt. Set aside.

3   In a large mixing bowl or stand mixer, mix the water, oil, and lemon juice on low.

4   Prepare the gelatin egg substitute. Add it to the wet ingredients and mix on medium-low speed just until combined.

5   Add the dry ingredients to the wet ingredients and mix until a thick dough forms.

6   Form five equal balls of dough and place them onto the lined baking sheet; press them down to form 1/2- to 3/4-inch-thick discs.

7   Bake for 12 minutes.

Bacon-Biscuit Variation:
Substitute bacon grease for the avocado oil and stir in four cooked and crumbled slices of bacon before baking.

Flatbread

Neutral in taste and versatile in use, this bread is perfect for sandwiches, pizzas, or in an olive oil dipping sauce!

🍴 Prep Time: 10 minutes   ⏰ Cooking Time: 12 minutes

🎁 Yield: One 10-inch circle

Ingredients:

1/3	cup arrowroot flour
1/3	cup coconut flour
1/2	teaspoon baking soda
3	tablespoons avocado oil
3	tablespoons water
1 1/2	teaspoons lemon juice
1	Gelatin Egg Substitute (page 18), prepared when directed

Directions:

1. Preheat the oven to 350°F.

2. In a small mixing bowl, combine the flours and baking soda. Set aside.

3. In a large mixing bowl or stand mixer, combine the oil, water, and lemon juice on low speed.

4. Prepare the gelatin egg substitute. Add it to the wet ingredients and mix on medium-low speed just until combined.

5. Add the dry ingredients to the wet ingredients and mix until a thick dough forms.

6. Prepare a 12-inch square sheet of parchment paper, and scrape the dough onto the paper. Roll out to form a 10-inch circle. If the dough cracks, sprinkle it with a bit of water and form the edges with hands after rolling. If dough sticks to the rolling pin, use a second piece of parchment paper over the top of the dough and use the rolling pin over the top of the paper. Transfer the bottom sheet of parchment paper, with the bread on top, to a circular baking sheet. If a top layer of parchment was used to roll, remove it before baking.

7. Bake for 12 minutes.

Focaccia Bread variation:
Prepare the bread as directed above. Before baking, brush evenly with 2 tablespoons of olive oil. Sprinkle the top with 1/2 teaspoon rosemary, 1/4 teaspoon garlic powder, and salt. Feel free to play with the herbs and seasonings depending on the flavor you desire!

Plantain Flatbread variation:
Substitute half of a peeled green plantain for the gelatin egg substitute. Follow the directions above, using a food processor instead of a mixer to process the ingredients.

Garlic Breadsticks

These little babies are absolutely delicious. The first time I made them, my non-paleo husband said, "Wow! These actually taste like real bread!" And the best part is that they're super quick and easy. In fact, you could whip these up every night of the week if you wanted to!

Prep Time: 10 minutes   **Cooking Time:** 10 minutes

Yield: 16 breadsticks

Ingredients:

2/3	cup coconut flour
2/3	cup arrowroot flour
3/4	teaspoon baking soda
1/2	teaspoon sea salt
1/2	cup avocado oil
1/3	cup water
2	teaspoons lemon juice
1	Gelatin Egg Substitute (page 18), prepared when directed
2	teaspoons dried or fresh rosemary (optional)

For the topping:

2	tablespoons avocado oil
1/4	teaspoon garlic powder
1/4	teaspoon sea salt

Directions:

1 Preheat the oven to 350°F and grease or line a baking sheet with parchment paper.

2 In a small bowl, mix together the flours, baking soda, and salt.

3 In a large mixing bowl or stand mixer, combine the oil, water, and lemon juice on low speed.

4 Prepare the gelatin egg substitute. Add it to the wet ingredients and mix on medium-low speed just until combined.

5 Add the dry ingredients to the wet ingredients and mix until a thick dough forms.

6 Scrape the dough onto another large sheet of parchment paper or nonstick surface. Divide it into sixteen golfball-sized pieces and roll each piece into a 6 to 8-inch stick. Transfer the sticks onto the prepared baking sheet.

7 For the topping, brush the sticks evenly with avocado oil. Sprinkle them with the garlic powder and salt.

8 Bake for 10 to 12 minutes, until the tops are golden brown.

Pita Bread

This pita bread can be sliced down the center for pita pockets or left unsliced for a wrap-style sandwich (gyros, anyone?). I have frozen these with success, but I've noticed they do become a bit brittle as time goes on.

🍴 Prep Time: 10 minutes   ⏰ Cooking Time: 12 minutes   🎁 Yield: 6 pita pockets

Ingredients:

1/3	cup arrowroot flour
1/3	cup coconut flour
1/2	teaspoon baking soda
3	tablespoons avocado oil
3	tablespoons water
1 1/2	teaspoons lemon juice
1	Gelatin Egg Substitute (page 18), prepared when directed

Directions:

1. Preheat the oven to 350°F and grease or line a baking sheet with parchment paper.

2. In a small bowl, mix together the flours and baking soda.

3. In a large mixing bowl or stand mixer, combine the oil, water, and lemon juice on low speed.

4. Prepare the gelatin egg substitute. Add it to the wet ingredients and mix on medium-low speed just until combined.

5. Add the dry ingredients to the wet ingredients and mix until a thick dough forms.

6. Scrape the dough onto a large sheet of parchment paper. Form it into three balls. Working with one ball at a time, place another sheet of parchment paper over the dough (to keep it from sticking to the rolling pin) and roll each ball into a 6-inch circle. Transfer the circles to the baking sheet. Bake for 12 minutes.

Let the pitas cool completely for 15 to 20 minutes on a wire rack. For pita pockets, use a sharp, serrated knife to cut the circles in half. Next, slice the cut side of each semicircle down the middle, leaving a 1/4 to 1/2-inch border along the edges. Store in the refrigerator for up to a week (or in the freezer for up to a month).

Tortillas

We live in South Texas, and "tortilla" was one of the first words out of our oldest son's mouth. Needless to say, we needed a replacement for our trusty staple. These are sneaky impostors that hold up to heavy fillings and are perfect for taco night.

Prep Time: 30 minutes   Cooking Time: 6 minutes   Yield: 12 tortillas

Ingredients:

2/3	cup coconut flour
2/3	cup arrowroot flour
1/2	tablespoon sea salt
1/4	teaspoon baking soda
1/3	cup lukewarm water
1/3	cup avocado oil
1 1/2	tablespoons lime juice
2	Gelatin Egg Substitutes (page 18), prepared when directed

Directions:

1 Preheat the oven to 350°F and line two baking sheets with parchment paper.

2 In a small mixing bowl, stir together the flours, salt, and baking soda.

3 In a large mixing bowl or stand mixer, mix the water, oil, and lime juice on low.

4 Prepare the gelatin egg substitute. Add it to the wet ingredients and mix on medium speed until combined.

5 Add the dry ingredients to the mixing bowl. Mix until completely combined.

6 Form twelve equal balls of dough. With a rolling pin, roll the balls flat to form 6-inch circles. If the dough sticks, roll it between two sheets of parchment paper.

7 Bake for 6 to 7 minutes, until the edges are just barely golden.

Tip:

When I make these, I rotate two baking sheets. I roll two tortillas and put them in the oven. While they're baking, I roll two more, place them on the second baking sheet, and pop them into the oven as well. Just remember to set a timer to keep track of which tortillas have been baking the longest!

Tortilla Chips:
Brush each tortilla with avocado oil, season with sea salt, and cut into wedges. Bake on a baking sheet at 350 for 18-20 minutes, flipping once, until crunchy.

Breakfasts

Tropical Green Smoothie

I never grow tired of this smoothie's fresh, tropical flavor! It also has a heaping amount of greens to add to your daily tally.

🍴 Prep Time: 5 minutes   🎁 Yield: 1 serving

Ingredients:

1/2	cup water
1	tablespoon coconut oil
2	tablespoons collagen, for added protein
1	cup frozen pineapple
1	banana, fresh or frozen
2	handfuls fresh baby spinach
1/4	lime, unpeeled

Directions:

Place all the ingredients in a blender and blend on high until smooth and creamy.

Creamy Chocolate Protein Smoothie

I often drink this smoothie on my on-the-go mornings. It is very filling, loaded with healthy fats and protein, and it is so creamy and delicious!

🍴 Prep Time: 5 minutes   🎁 Yield: 1 serving

Ingredients:

1	cup crushed ice
1/2	cup coconut milk
1/2	medium avocado, peeled and seeded
1	banana, fresh or frozen
2	tablespoons collagen, for added protein
2	tablespoons honey
1	tablespoon carob powder
1	teaspoon ground cinnamon

Directions:

Place all the ingredients in a blender and blend on high until smooth and creamy.

Pumpkin Pie Smoothie

I love to start the day with this nutrient-packed smoothie. It's perfect year-round, but it's especially crave-worthy when fall rolls in! Loaded with a half cup of pumpkin, it provides your entire daily serving of vitamin A, which supports immune function, as well as a generous helping of potassium and magnesium. When I'm using this as a quick breakfast, I always add two tablespoons of collagen powder for a protein boost.

🍴 Prep Time: 5 minutes 　　　🎁 Yield: 1 serving

Ingredients:

1/2	cup pumpkin puree
1/2	cup coconut milk
1	banana, fresh or frozen
1	cup crushed ice
1/2	teaspoon ground cinnamon
1/4	teaspoon ground ginger
1/8	teaspoon ground cloves
2	tablespoons collagen, for added protein
1	tablespoon honey or maple syrup

Directions:

Place all the ingredients in a blender and blend on high until smooth and creamy.

Strawberry–Banana Morning Milkshake

This is one of my kids' favorite treats, and it's one I can enjoy, too! Pair this with Breakfast Sausage (page 59) in the morning or enjoy after dinner as a dessert!

🍴 Prep Time: 5 minutes 　　　🎁 Yield: 4 serving

Ingredients:

1	(10-ounce) package of frozen strawberries
1	banana, fresh or frozen
1	cup coconut milk
1/2	cup crushed ice
2	tablespoons collagen (optional for added protein)
1	tablespoon honey (optional)

Directions:

Place all the ingredients in a blender and blend on high until smooth and creamy.

Lox and Cado

This easy dish is one I enjoy often for breakfast or as a snack. It's a simple and delicious combination of salty and sour flavors, and it's also full of nutrients and omega-3 fatty acids!

Prep Time: 5 minutes   Yield: 4 servings

Ingredients:

1   (8-ounce) package of sliced smoked salmon

2   avocados, peeled, seeded, and halved

2   teaspoons lemon juice

2   teaspoons capers

Directions:

Lay the smoked salmon slices over the avocado halves. Sprinkle with lemon juice and capers. Serve immediately.

Breakfast Sausage

One of the hardest things about starting this diet was giving up my morning eggs. I wanted something to fill me up and provide enough protein to last me until lunchtime. This recipe deliciously fits the bill and can be made on Sunday to give you high-protein breakfasts for the entire week.

Prep Time: 10 minutes   Cooking Time: 10 minutes

Yield: 6 servings

Ingredients:

2   tablespoons coconut oil

1   pound ground pork

1   tablespoon maple syrup

1   teaspoon sea salt

1   teaspoon dried rubbed sage

1   teaspoon dried parsley

1/2   teaspoon dried thyme

1/4   teaspoon ground cloves

Directions:

1   Melt the oil in a large skillet over medium heat.

2   In a stand mixer or by hand, mix the maple syrup and seasonings into the ground pork.

3   **For patties:** Shape into 6 patties, about 4 inches in diameter and 1/3-inch thick. Fry patties for 3 to 5 minutes on each side until cooked throughout and well browned.

For crumbled sausage: Crumble the pork into the hot oil and cook until browned throughout, stirring occasionally.

For meatballs: Preheat the oven to 350°F. Grease or line a baking sheet with parchment paper. Scoop out 1 tablespoon of the pork mixture at a time to make 24 meatballs.   Arrange the meatballs evenly on the sheet and bake for 20 minutes.

Bacon–Maple Salmon

Quick and simple, this recipe is a protein-packed and delicious one to add to your morning routine! For the best flavor, marinate the salmon overnight, or simply brush the marinade on in the morning for a last-minute breakfast.

Prep Time: 5 minutes

Cooking Time: 15 minutes

Marinate Time: Overnight (optional)

Yield: 4 servings

Ingredients:

4	salmon filets
2	tablespoons maple syrup
2	tablespoons Balsamic vinegar
1/2	teaspoon dried rubbed sage
4	slices uncooked bacon, halved

Directions:

1 The night before serving, place salmon filets, maple syrup, and Balsamic vinegar in a sealed container in the refrigerator to marinate. Gently shake to mix liquid and coat salmon

2 In the morning, preheat the oven to 425°F. Grease or line a baking sheet with parchment paper.

3 Arrange the salmon filets on a baking sheet. If not marinated, mix the maple syrup and Balsamic vinegar in a small dish. Brush or drizzle onto the salmon filets.

4 Lay two halves of bacon slices lengthwise on top of each filet. Sprinkle all the filets evenly with the sage.

5 Place the baking sheet in the third of the oven closest to the heat source and bake for 15 minutes until the center of the salmon is flaky and opaque. Serve hot.

Cinnamon Pork & Apples

This dish is absolutely delicious! My whole family loves it, and I love serving a protein-packed breakfast to start our days.

🍴 Prep Time: 10 minutes   ⏰ Cooking Time: 15 minutes

🎁 Yield: 4 servings

Ingredients:

2   tablespoons coconut oil

1   pound boneless pork chops, cubed

1   teaspoon ground cinnamon

1/2   teaspoon sea salt

1/4   teaspoon dried rubbed sage

1/4   teaspoon dried thyme

1/8   teaspoon ground cloves

3   apples, cored and sliced

2   tablespoons maple syrup

Directions:

1   In a large skillet, heat the coconut oil over medium heat.

2   Add the pork chops to the skillet and season with the cinnamon, salt, sage, thyme, and cloves. Brown the chops for 4 to 5 minutes, stirring to sear all sides.

3   Add the apples, drizzling the apples and the pork chops with maple syrup. Stir all the ingredients together and sauté for 10 to 12 more minutes, stirring occasionally until the apples are tender. Serve with the juices from the bottom of the pan spooned over the top.

Pigs in a Pillow

A perfect grab-and-go breakfast, this twist on "pigs in a blanket" is a filling treat. Drizzled with a touch of maple syrup, these are great to eat right away or to freeze and reheat.

Prep Time: 20 minutes   Cooking Time: 30 minutes   Yield: 24 mini muffins

Ingredients:

1   recipe Breakfast Sausage Meatballs (page 59), uncooked

1/2   cup avocado oil

1/3   cup water

2/3   cup coconut flour

2/3   cup arrowroot flour

3/4   teaspoon baking soda

1/2   teaspoon sea salt

2   teaspoons lemon juice

1   Gelatin Egg Substitute (page 18), prepared when directed

Directions:

1. Preheat the oven to 350°F and lightly grease a 24-cup mini muffin tin with coconut oil. Grease or line a baking sheet with parchment paper as well.

2. Arrange the uncooked meatballs on the parchment-lined baking sheet and bake for 20 minutes.

3. Meanwhile, prepare the "pillows." Place all the ingredients except for the gelatin egg substitute in a large mixing bowl or stand mixer.

4. Prepare the gelatin egg substitute and add it to the mixing bowl. Beat on medium speed until a thick dough forms.

5. Scoop out the dough, 1 tablespoon at a time, and roll into balls. Place one ball into each mini muffin cup. Set aside.

6. When the meatballs are finished baking, press one into each unbaked "pillow." Shape the dough around the meatballs with fingertips, if desired.

7. Bake for 10 to 12 minutes until the edges of the muffins are golden brown.

Breakfasts

63

Breakfast Pâté

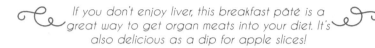

If you don't enjoy liver, this breakfast pâté is a great way to get organ meats into your diet. It's also delicious as a dip for apple slices!

🍴 Prep Time: 5 minutes   ⏰ Cooking Time: 15 minutes

🎁 Yield: 1 1/2 cups

Ingredients:

1/2	cup bacon grease
1	medium onion, coarsely chopped
1	teaspoon dried rubbed sage
1	teaspoon dried parsley
1/2	teaspoon dried thyme
1/2	teaspoon sea salt
1/4	teaspoon ground cloves
1	pound chicken livers, rinsed and patted dry
2	tablespoons maple syrup

Directions:

1. In a large skillet, heat the bacon grease over medium heat. Add the onion and seasonings and sauté for 5 to 7 minutes until softened and golden brown.

2. Gently push the onion aside in the skillet and add the livers to the pan. Sauté for 5 minutes on each side, or until browned on the outside and pink in the center. Remove the skillet from the heat, cover, and let sit for 5 minutes.

3. Pour the liver mixture into a food processor. Add the maple syrup and process until smooth and creamy.

Sweet Potato Hash Browns

A perfect complement to Breakfast Sausage (page 59) or Bacon-Maple Salmon (page 61), these hash browns are simple, filling, and to die for!

🍴 Prep Time: 15 minutes   ⏰ Cooking Time: 20 minutes

👥 Yield: 6 servings

Ingredients:

4   slices bacon, coarsely chopped

5   cups shredded sweet potato (about 2 large sweet potatoes)

1/2   teaspoon garlic powder

Directions:

1   In a large skillet, cook the bacon on medium heat until most of its fat is rendered, about 6 to 7 minutes. Remove the bacon and set aside.

2   Add the sweet potatoes and garlic powder to the hot bacon grease. Sauté for 10 to 15 minutes, stirring occasionally, until the sweet potatoes are fork tender.

Hot N'oatmeal

If you are looking for a sweet plant-based recipe that you can eat in the mornings, this is it! Serve it to a crowd, or scoop it out and reheat a little each day!

Prep Time: 10 minutes   Cooking Time: 5 minutes

Yield: 6 servings

Ingredients:

1   medium spaghetti or 2 acorn squash, cooked, peeled, and seeded

1   cup coconut milk

2   tablespoons honey

2   teaspoons ground cinnamon

Directions:

Place all the ingredients in a food processor. Pulse until the consistency is similar to oatmeal. Reheat if necessary.

Variations:

Cinnamon-Raisin: Stir in an extra teaspoon of cinnamon plus 1/4 cup raisins.

Warm Maple-Banana: Omit the honey. Stir in one quartered and sliced banana and 2 tablespoons of maple syrup.

Berries and Cream: Stir in 1 cup berries, fresh or frozen and thawed.

Peaches and Cream: Stir in an additional teaspoon of cinnamon and 1 cup chopped peaches, fresh or frozen and thawed.

Egg-Free Breakfast Skillet

Whether you're cooking for friends and family or making a breakfast to eat throughout the week, this meal is delicious and satisfying.

🍴 Prep Time: 10 minutes   ⏰ Cooking Time: 20 minutes

👥 Yield: 6 servings

Ingredients:

2   tablespoons avocado oil

1   pound sweet potato or butternut squash, peeled and cubed

2   medium zucchini, quartered and sliced

1/2   cup chopped onion

1/2   teaspoon sea salt

1/4   teaspoon garlic powder

2   handfuls baby spinach

1   recipe Breakfast Sausage, cooked and crumbled (page 59)

Directions:

1   In a large skillet, add the avocado oil over medium heat. Add the sweet potatoes or squash, zucchini, onion, sea salt, and garlic powder. Sauté for 15 minutes, or until the sweet potatoes or butternut squash are just fork tender. Stir occasionally to ensure even cooking.

2   Add the spinach and sausage to the skillet. Sauté until the spinach is wilted and the sausage is heated through, about 4-5 minutes. Serve hot.

Soups, Salads, & Sides

Cole Slaw

Sweet, salty, and with a tangy crunch, this dish is a winner at a picnic or barbecue for all you non-paleo friends!

🍴	Prep Time: 10 minutes	⏰	Cooking Time: 5 minutes

🎁 Yield: 6-8 servings

Ingredients:

2	tablespoons evaporated cane juice
1	tablespoon lemon juice
1/3	cup avocado oil
1	tablespoon palm shortening
1	tablespoon apple cider vinegar
1/4	teaspoon sea salt
4	slices bacon, cooked, cooled and crumbled
6	cups slaw mix (prepackaged or a homemade combination of shredded green cabbage, purple cabbage and carrots)

Directions:

1   In a small saucepan over medium heat, dissolve the evaporated cane juice into the lemon juice to create a syrup. Do not let boil. Transfer to a mixing bowl and mix on high speed until completely cool to the touch.

2   Add the oil, shortening, vinegar, and salt to the syrup. Beat on high speed until creamy.

3   Stir the bacon into the slaw mix and pour the dressing over the slaw mix. Toss to combine and serve cold.

Spiced Cranberry Relish

This sauce is perfect for a holiday gathering or for slathering on top of a turkey burger! The combination of orange, cloves, and sea salt in this dish adds a crave-worthy depth of flavor.

Prep Time: 2 minutes   Cooking Time: 12 minutes

Chilling Time: 4 hours   Yield: 2 1/2 cups

Ingredients:

3/4   cup honey

1/3   cup freshly squeezed orange juice

1/3   cup water

1/4   teaspoon ground cloves

1/8   teaspoon sea salt

12   ounces fresh cranberries

Directions:

1   In a medium saucepan, combine the honey, orange juice, water, cloves, and salt.

2   Bring the mixture to a boil. Add the cranberries and return to a boil. Decrease the heat to medium-low and boil gently for 10 minutes. Transfer to a serving bowl and refrigerate for 4 hours until completely cool and gelled.

Tuna Salad

This tuna salad is packed with protein, healthy fats, and crunchy vegetables! I love serving this "lettuce boat style" in crisp romaine leaves.

Prep Time: 10 minutes   Yield: 4 servings

Ingredients:

2   (6-ounce) cans tuna, drained

1/3   cup Creamy Egg-Free Mayo (page 35) or mashed avocado

1/3   cup chopped celery

1/3   cup diced red onion

1/2   teaspoon dried dill

1/4   cup sliced Kalamata olives (optional)

Directions:

In a medium mixing bowl, stir all the ingredients together until uniform throughout. Serve over greens, on a lettuce boat, or in Pita Bread (page 52).

Chicken Salad

I have always loved chicken salad, and I especially love to make a big batch of it to eat for lunches throughout the week! This medley of chicken, green onions, grapes, and creamy mayo makes for a perfect blend of flavors and textures for a delicious lunch.

Prep Time: 10 minutes   Yield: 4 servings

Ingredients:

2   cups cooked chopped chicken, completely cooled

1/3   cup Creamy Egg-Free Mayo (page 35) or mashed avocado

1/3   cup grapes halved

1/3   cup sliced green onions

1/2   teaspoon dried dill weed

1/4   teaspoon garlic powder

Directions:

In a medium mixing bowl, stir all the ingredients together until uniform throughout. Serve over greens, on a lettuce boat, or in Pita Bread (page 52).

Tips:

Leftover chicken or an unseasoned rotisserie chicken makes this recipe extremely fast and easy!

Italian Pastaless Salad

This recipe is based on a spaghetti salad my mom made when I was growing up. The first time I made the paleo version, I reminded myself before I took the first bite that it wouldn't be quite as good as the salad I remembered. I was very wrong! I actually loved the crisp noodles and flavors of the vegetables so much more than a wheat-based pasta salad.

Prep Time: 15 minutes	Yield: 8 servings

Ingredients:

For the salad:

2 1/2	pounds zucchini squash, peeled and spiral-cut or julienne-cut into noodles
1/2	cup sliced green onions
1/2	large cucumber, quartered and sliced
1/2	cup halved kalamata or black olives

For the dressing:

1/2	cup olive oil
3	tablespoons apple cider vinegar
1 1/2	teaspoons dried oregano
3/4	teaspoon onion powder
3/4	teaspoon dried parsley
3/4	teaspoon sea salt
1/2	teaspoon garlic powder
1/2	teaspoon dried basil
1/8	teaspoon dried thyme

Directions:

1. Place all the veggies in a large bowl.

2. Place all the dressing ingredients in a small glass jar. Shake to mix thoroughly. Pour the dressing over the vegetables and toss to combine. Serve cold.

Soups, Salads, & Sides

73

Wedge Salad with Bacon & Ranch Dressing

A wedge salad is one of my favorite pre-dinner salads. It looks so impressive when set before your family or guests, but with little chopping, it is one of the easiest and fastest salads to prepare!

🍴 Prep Time: 15 minutes   🎁 Yield: 6 servings

Ingredients:

1	large head iceberg lettuce, cut into 6 wedges
1	small red onion, sliced
1/2	pound bacon, cooked and crumbled
1/2	cup sliced Kalamata olives
1	recipe Ranch Dressing (page 39)

Directions:

Arrange lettuce wedges on six salad plates. Top each wedge with onion, bacon, and olives. Drizzle the dressing over the top.

Autumn Butternut Bisque

In college, a little café by our campus served a butternut squash soup that I often turned to when finals hit. It offered a warm bowl of comfort on those long days of studying. While I'm certain it was loaded with ingredients I can no longer tolerate, this version provides that same flavor, smooth consistency, and comforting goodness. I love to make a big batch of this and eat it for lunch throughout the week.

🍴 Prep Time: 10 minutes　　⏰ Cooking time: 12 minutes

🎁 Yield: 4 servings

Ingredients:

1　(15-ounce) can butternut squash purée (or 4 cups cubed, boiled, and puréed)

1　(13.5-ounce) can coconut milk

1　cup julienned carrots

2　tablespoons honey

1/2　teaspoon garlic powder

1/2　teaspoon orange zest, fresh or dried

1/2　teaspoon sea salt

Directions:

In a large saucepan or pot, whisk all the ingredients together. Bring to a boil and reduce heat. Simmer for 10 minutes, or until the carrots are soft. Serve hot.

Broccoli-Cheddar Soup

Believe it or not, broccoli-cheddar soup doesn't always have to be made with dairy. This recipe uses the ever-versatile cauliflower to create a cheesy, creamy soup that is chock-full of healing nutrients.

🍴 Prep Time: 15 minutes   ⏰ Cooking Time: 20 minutes

🎁 Yield: 6 servings

Ingredients:

6	cups cauliflower florets, fresh or frozen
1	cup peeled and chopped carrots, fresh or frozen
2	cups Bone Broth (page 19)
1/3	cup avocado oil
1/4	cup nutritional yeast
1/2	teaspoon onion powder
1/2	teaspoon sea salt
3	cups broccoli florets, fresh or frozen
6	slices bacon, cooked and crumbled

Directions:

1. Fill a large pot halfway with water and bring it to a boil. Add the cauliflower and carrots, and boil for 15 minutes, or until tender.

2. Using a slotted spoon, remove the cooked cauliflower and carrots and add them to a blender, reserving the water in the pot. Add the broth, oil, nutritional yeast, onion powder, and salt to the blender and liquefy.

3. Return the same pot of water to a boil and add the broccoli, boiling until tender. When finished, drain and discard the water, keeping the broccoli in the pot.

4. Pour the blended mixture over the broccoli in the pot. Cook over medium until the soup is heated through. Garnish with bacon.

Crab Bisque

This savory and filling soup tastes as if it takes a lot of time and effort, but it's actually very simple and quick to make. Although it can be a meal by itself, I love to serve it with warm crab legs for a special treat!

Prep Time: 10 minutes   Cooking Time: 20 minutes

Yield: 6 servings

Ingredients:

2	tablespoons avocado oil
1	pound baby carrots or chopped carrots
1	large yellow onion, coarsely chopped
2	cloves garlic, coarsely chopped
4	cups Bone Broth (page 19)
1	(13.5-ounce) can coconut milk
1	tablespoon lemon juice
1	pound cooked crab meat
1 1/2	teaspoons sea salt
2	tablespoons chopped chives, fresh or dried

Directions:

1. In a large pot over medium-high heat, sauté carrots, onions, and garlic in the avocado oil for 10 minutes until lightly browned.

2. Add the broth and the coconut milk. Bring to a boil and reduce heat to medium-low. Cover and simmer until carrots are soft, about 10 minutes.

3. Using an immersion blender (or carefully transferring to a blender in batches), blend the mixture until creamy. Add the remaining ingredients and return to the stove top until heated through.

Fried Cauliflower Rice

This "cauli-rice" mixture is wonderful with Asian Lettuce Wraps (page 94) or Teriyaki Chicken Tenders (page 95). To make this a complete meal, you can even cook chopped chicken breasts in the oil before adding the cauliflower to the skillet.

Prep Time: 15 minutes   Cooking Time: 12 minutes   Yield: 4-6 servings

Ingredients:

1	head cauliflower, stem removed and coarsely chopped
2	tablespoons avocado oil
1/2	cup sliced onion
1	large carrot, thinly sliced
1	medium zucchini, coarsely chopped
1/2	cup coconut aminos
1	teaspoon fish sauce
2	cloves garlic, peeled and minced
1	teaspoon sea salt

Directions:

1 Place the cauliflower florets into a food processor. Pulse until the cauliflower has turned into rice-size granules. Set aside.

2 Heat the oil in a large skillet over medium-high heat. Add the onion, carrot and zucchini to the skillet and stir-fry for 5 minutes. Add in the coconut aminos, fish sauce, garlic, and salt. Stir to combine.

3 Add the cauliflower to the skillet. Stir the cauliflower into the vegetable mixture and stir-fry for 5 to 7 more minutes, until the cauli-rice is tender and semi-translucent.

Roasted Chicken & Vegetable Soup

Warm and comforting on a chilly day, this soup has a great old-fashioned flavor.

🍴 Prep Time: 15 minutes ⏰ Cooking Time: 20 minutes 🎁 Yield: 6 servings

Ingredients:

2 tablespoons avocado oil

1/2 head green cabbage, coarsely chopped

4 medium carrots, sliced

1 medium onion, coarsely chopped

1 zucchini, quartered and sliced

1 clove garlic, minced

1 teaspoon dried thyme

1 teaspoon sea salt

2-3 cups shredded, cooked chicken

4 cups Bone Broth (page 19)

Directions:

1 In a large pot, heat the avocado oil over medium-high heat. Add the cabbage, carrots, onion, zucchini, garlic, thyme, and salt. Sauté for 10 minutes, stirring occasionally, until browned.

2 Add the chicken and broth and bring to a boil. Reduce the heat to low and simmer for 10 to 20 minutes.

Bacon-Sautéed Asparagus

Salty and savory, this bacon-infused side dish beautifully complements a hearty steak or grilled chicken.

Prep Time: 2 minutes   Cooking Time: 20 minutes   Yield: 4 servings

Ingredients:

4	slices bacon, coarsely chopped
1	pound fresh asparagus
1/2	teaspoon garlic powder

Directions:

1   In a large skillet over medium heat, cook the bacon until most of its fat is rendered, about 7 to 9 minutes.

2   Add the asparagus, season with the garlic powder, and stir to coat. Let simmer for 10 to 15 minutes, stirring occasionally, until desired tenderness is reached.

Brussels Sprouts with Bacon and Cranberries

I happen to really love Brussels sprouts, but I also realize that not everyone shares that sentiment. However, when cooked with salty bacon and blitzed with dried cranberries just before serving, this recipe convinced even my family that they really could enjoy Brussels sprouts.

🍴 Prep Time: 5 minutes   ⏰ Cooking Time: 20 minutes   🎁 Yield: 4 servings

Ingredients:

4   slices bacon, coarsely chopped

1   pound fresh Brussels sprouts, trimmed
     and halved

1/4 cup dried cranberries (look for organic
     varieties that use evaporated cane juice
     instead of refined sugar)

Directions:

1   In a large skillet over medium-high heat, cook
     the bacon until most of the fat is rendered,
     about 7 to 9 minutes. Stir to prevent burning.

2   Add the Brussels sprouts to the hot pan
     and cook until they're browned and crispy
     on the edges, about 10 to 12 minutes. Stir
     occasionally.

3   Add the cranberries and stir to combine. Cook
     for 1 to 2 more minutes to heat cranberries
     through, stirring occasionally.

Cheesy Cauliflower Rice

Nutritional yeast is a saving grace when it comes to cheese cravings. This savory side is a wonderful complement to any entrée.

Prep Time: 7 minutes   Cooking Time: 25 minutes

Yield: 4-6 servings

Ingredients:

1	head cauliflower, stemmed
1/3	cup coconut milk
1/4	cup sliced green onions
2	tablespoons nutritional yeast
3/4	teaspoon sea salt
2	tablespoons avocado oil

Directions:

1   Place the cauliflower into a food processor. Pulse until the cauliflower resembles grains of rice. Set aside.

2   In a small bowl, whisk together the coconut milk, green onions, nutritional yeast, and salt. Set aside.

3   Heat the oil in a large skillet over medium heat. Add the cauliflower and sauté for 5 minutes, stirring frequently.

4   Add the coconut milk mixture to the cauliflower, stirring to coat. Set the heat to low, cover, and cook for 15 to 20 minutes, until the cauliflower is tender and semi translucent.

Fauxtato Salad

I love potato salad with burgers or Peach-Braised Short Ribs (page 108) on a summer day! This recipe omits the potatoes and adds their veggie impostor, cauliflower, which is coated with a creamy dressing.

🍴 Prep Time: 10 minutes　　⏰ Cooking Time: 5 minutes　　🎁 Yield: 6-8 servings

Ingredients:

For the salad:

1　pound cauliflower, cut into 1/2-inch pieces (about 4 cups)

1/3　cup diced red onion

3　tablespoons finely chopped cucumbers

3　slices bacon, cooled and crumbled

For the dressing:

1/3　cup avocado oil

2　tablespoons palm shortening

2　teaspoons apple cider vinegar

1　teaspoon dried parsley

1/2　teaspoon dried dill

1/2　teaspoon sea salt

1/4　teaspoon ground turmeric

Directions:

1　In a large saucepan, bring water to a boil. Once boiling, add the cauliflower and boil for 5 minutes. Immediately drain the cauliflower and rinse with cold water to stop the cooking process.

2　In a large bowl, combine the cooked cauliflower, red onion, cucumbers, and bacon. Set aside.

3　Prepare the dressing by combining the avocado oil, palm shortening, vinegar, parsley, dill, sea salt, and turmeric in a mixing bowl or stand mixer.

4　Stir the dressing into the vegetable mixture until completely coated. Serve cold and store in the refrigerator.

Mashed Fauxtatoes

Giving up mashed potatoes wasn't easy for me. They've always been one of my favorite foods, and this recipe is a great replacement!

🍴 Prep Time: 15 minutes	⏰ Cooking Time: 25 minutes	🎁 Yield: 4-6 servings

Ingredients:

1 head cauliflower, stemmed and cut into large florets

1 medium white-fleshed sweet potato or parsnip, peeled and coarsely chopped

3 garlic cloves, halved

1 tablespoon olive oil

1 teaspoon sea salt

Directions:

1 Bring a large pot of water to a boil. Add the cauliflower, sweet potato or parsnip, and garlic and boil for 20 minutes, until the vegetables are fork tender.

2 Drain the vegetables and discard the water, shaking off as much liquid as possible. Return cooked vegetables to the pot.

3 Add the olive oil and salt. Blend with a hand mixer or immersion blender until smooth.

Variation:

Loaded Mashed Fauxtatoes Variation: Once mashed fauxtatoes are finished, stir in 1 tablespoon nutritional yeast, 5 slices bacon (cooked and crumbled), and 1/4 cup sliced green onions. Garnish with additional bacon and green onions, if desired.

Roasted Sweet Potatoes

A delightful side dish to accompany nearly any main course these sweet potatoes add a simple and delicious starch to round out a meal.

🍴 Prep Time: 10 minutes   ⏰ Cooking Time: 25 minutes

⏰ Yield: 4 servings

Ingredients:

1 1/2   pounds sweet potatoes, chopped into 1/2-inch pieces

1   medium yellow onion, coarsely chopped

3   tablespoons avocado oil

1   teaspoon dried rosemary

        sea salt

Directions:

1   Preheat the oven to 425°F. Grease or line a baking sheet with parchment paper.

2   Place the chopped sweet potatoes, onions, and rosemary onto the baking sheet. Drizzle avocado oil over the top and toss to coat. Season with salt to taste. Bake for 25 minutes until fork tender.

Scalloped Sweet Potatoes

This side dish is perfect for a dinner party or holiday gathering. Rosemary infuses a lovely flavor throughout this entire dish.

🍴 Prep Time: 15 minutes   ⏰ Cooking Time: 40 minutes

⏱ Yield: 8 servings

Ingredients:

2   pounds sweet potatoes, sliced 1/4-inch thick (about 3 medium potatoes)

1/2   medium yellow onion, sliced 1/8-inch thick

1   (13.5-ounce) can coconut milk

1/2   teaspoon garlic powder

1   teaspoon sea salt

1/2   teaspoon dried rosemary

Directions:

1   Preheat the oven to 350°F.

2   Layer the sweet potatoes and onion in an ungreased 3-quart casserole dish.

3   Whisk the remaining ingredients together and pour over the sweet potatoes and onions.

4   Bake uncovered for 40 minutes. If desired, finish by turning the broiler on for the last 3 to 5 minutes, until the top is browned.

Entrées

These recipes are 30-minute meals

Roasted Chicken over Hearty Vegetables

This is one of my all-time favorite meals and one of our family staples. I love the savory chicken, the roasted vegetables, and the slightly charred cabbage. It all adds up to a delicate marriage of flavors that is deeply satisfying. This meal is also cooked in one dish, which means cleanup is a breeze. And because of its gorgeous presentation, this is a meal I often serve to dinner guests. The photo for this entrée is on previous page.

🍴 Prep Time: 15 minutes　　　　⏰ Cooking Time: 90 minutes　　　　🎁 Yield: 6 servings

Ingredients:

1	large yellow onion, cut into 2-inch pieces
2-3	white-fleshed sweet potatoes, cut into 2-inch pieces
5	large carrots, cut into 2-inch pieces
1/2	large head green cabbage, cut into 2-inch pieces
1	whole chicken, innards removed, rinsed and patted dry
1	head garlic, cut in half
1	lemon, cut in half
1/2	bunch fresh thyme
1	tablespoon avocado oil
	sea salt

Directions:

1 Preheat the oven to 425°F.

2 Place the onion, potatoes, carrots, and cabbage in the bottom of a 9 by 13-inch or larger casserole dish.

3 Stuff the garlic, lemon, and thyme into the cavity of the chicken. Tie the legs, if desired for presentation.

4 Lay the chicken on top of the bed of vegetables, breast-side up.

5 Rub the oil onto the chicken skin and season with salt to taste.

6 Roast, uncovered, for 90 minutes, or until the internal temperature reaches 165°F. Let rest for 10 minutes before carving.

Herb-Roasted Drumsticks

My kids love drumsticks. Something about eating with no utensils must really appeal to them. This is a quick and simple dinner we enjoy often. Throw the drumsticks on the grill or in the oven—either way, you can't go wrong!

🍴 Prep Time: 5 minutes   ⏰ Cooking Time: 40 minutes

⏰ Yield: 4-6 servings

Ingredients:

10   chicken drumsticks, skin on or skinless

1/2   teaspoon sea salt

1/2   teaspoon garlic powder

1/2   teaspoon onion powder

1/2   teaspoon dried oregano

1/2   teaspoon dried parsley

1/2   teaspoon dried rosemary

1/2   teaspoon dried thyme

Directions:

1   Preheat the oven to 375°F or the grill to medium-low heat. Arrange drumsticks on a baking sheet.

2   In a small bowl, mix the remaining ingredients together. Sprinkle evenly over the drumsticks, rubbing in as needed.

3   Bake or grill for 40 minutes, turning once.

Oven-Fried Chicken Breasts

These oven-fried chicken breasts are crispy on the outside, tender in the center, and full of flavor. If you're craving a comfort meal from your past or trying to feed a non-paleo loved one, this one should do the trick.

🍴 Prep Time: 5 minutes   ⏰ Cooking Time: 25 minutes   🎁 Yield: 4-6 servings

Ingredients:

1/3   cup avocado oil

1/3   cup shredded, unsweetened coconut

2   tablespoons coconut flour

2   tablespoons arrowroot flour

2   teaspoons sea salt

1   teaspoon dried parsley

1   teaspoon garlic powder

1/2   teaspoon onion powder

4   boneless skinless chicken breasts, patted dry

Directions:

1   Preheat the oven to 400°F and grease or line a baking sheet with parchment paper.

2   Pour the oil into a pie plate or shallow dish. In a separate pie plate or shallow dish, mix the shredded coconut, flours, salt, parsley, garlic powder, and onion powder together.

3   Dredge the breasts through the oil, then through the flour mixture.

4   Arrange the breasts on the baking sheet and bake, uncovered, for 25 to 30 minutes, or until they're golden brown and the internal temperature reaches 165°F. To brown the breading more, turn on the broiler for 2-4 minutes - watching carefully to avoid burning - until the coating has darkened to the preferred color.

Stacked Chicken Enchiladas Verdes

 No need to miss out on great Mexican food when these are on the menu!

Prep Time: 15 minutes   **Cooking Time:** 40 minutes

Yield: 12 servings

Ingredients:

1	pound orange or white-fleshed sweet potatoes, peeled
3	cups shredded, cooked chicken
3/4	cup Bone Broth (page 19)
1/2	medium white onion
1/2	bunch cilantro
1/3	cup diced avocado
3	cloves garlic, peeled
2	tablespoons lime juice
1	teaspoon sea salt
	white onion, diced for garnish (optional)
	chopped cilantro for garnish (optional)

Directions:

1   Preheat the oven to 375°F and grease an 8-inch square baking dish.

2   Slice the peeled potatoes lengthwise to 1/8-inch thickness to create long thin tortilla-like strips (This is done most easily with a mandolin slicer). Set aside.

3   In a blender, purée the broth, onion, cilantro, avocado, garlic, lime juice, and salt. Set aside.

4   Layer one third of the sweet potatoes in the baking dish. Spread half of the chicken over the potatoes and top with a third of the green sauce. Repeat, ending with a layer of sweet potatoes and spreading the remaining green sauce over the top.

5   Cover the dish with aluminum foil and bake for 40 minutes, until a toothpick is easily inserted in the center.

Asian Lettuce Wraps

30-Minute Meal

Every time I make this meal, my husband and oldest son claim it's their favorite. This dinner is light, flavorful, and full of healthy meat and vegetables.

Prep Time: 10 minutes   Cooking Time: 20 minutes   Yield: 8 servings

Ingredients:

3   tablespoons heat-stable cooking oil

2   boneless skinless chicken breasts, diced

1/3   cup coconut aminos

2   tablespoons honey

2   cloves garlic, minced

2   teaspoons apple cider vinegar

1/2   teaspoon sea salt

1 1/2   cups minced mushrooms

1   (5-ounce) can diced water chestnuts, rinsed and drained

1/3   cup chopped green onions

8   iceberg lettuce leaves

1   package kelp noodles (optional for topping)

Directions:

1   In a large skillet over medium-high heat, heat the oil. Add the chicken and coconut aminos and cook for 5 minutes, stirring frequently.

2   Add the honey, garlic, vinegar, and salt. Stir to coat the chicken. Add the mushrooms, water chestnuts, and green onion and stir-fry for 3 to 4 minutes, until the mushrooms are soft. Simmer over medium-high heat until the liquid has evaporated, about 10 to 12 more minutes, stirring occasionally to prevent burning.

3   Spoon the filling onto the lettuce leaves and eat taco-style. Serve with extra coconut aminos and kelp noodles, if desired.

Tip:

Simplify this recipe by substituting 1 pound of ground chicken for the diced chicken breasts.

Teriyaki Chicken Tenders with Sautéed Broccoli

30-Minute Meal

Sweet and salty is always a good combination. These chicken tenders are easy to prepare, and with a simple side, this quick meal is perfect for a weeknight dinner. Feel free to add a side of Roasted Sweet Potatoes (page 86) for a more filling meal.

Prep Time: 15 minutes   Cooking Time: 15 minutes   Yield: 4 servings

Ingredients:

For the chicken:

1	pound chicken tenders (optionally threaded onto kabob sticks)
1/3	cup coconut aminos
2	tablespoons honey
1/2	teaspoon fish sauce
1	tablespoon dried chives
1/2	teaspoon garlic powder
1/2	teaspoon ground ginger
1/4	teaspoon sea salt

For the broccoli:

2	tablespoons avocado oil
1	pound fresh or frozen broccoli florets
1/4	teaspoon sea salt

Directions:

1   Preheat the oven to 425°F. Grease or line a baking sheet with parchment paper.

2   Arrange the chicken tenders on the baking sheet. In a small mixing bowl, whisk together the coconut aminos, honey, fish sauce, chives, garlic, ginger, and salt. Brush the mixture onto the chicken. Bake for 15 to 20 minutes, or until the internal temperature reaches 165°F.

3   Meanwhile, pour the avocado oil into a large skillet and heat over medium-high heat. Add the broccoli and salt and sauté for 15 minutes, stirring occasionally. Serve hot alongside the chicken tenders.

Entrées

95

White Lasagna with Turkey and Zucchini

Filling and full of nutrients and flavors, this white lasagna is a wonderful dish! As with traditional lasagna, the end result is well worth the effort! Prepare this ahead of time and pop it in the oven for an easy weeknight dinner.

🍴 Prep Time: 30 minutes   ⏰ Cooking Time: 1 hour   🎁 Yield: 4-6 servings

Ingredients:

1   pound white-fleshed sweet potatoes, peeled (If you can find a single, 1-pound sweet potato, this makes the "noodles" look very realistic.)

2   tablespoons avocado oil, plus an additional 2 tablespoons for the nutritional yeast mixture

1   pound ground turkey

1/2 teaspoon sea salt, plus an additional 1/2 teaspoon for seasoning the squash mixture

2   cups julienned or shredded yellow squash (about 1 squash)

2   cups julienned or shredded zucchini (about 1 zucchini)

6   cloves garlic, minced

1   tablespoon chopped fresh oregano or 1 teaspoon dried oregano

1   tablespoon chopped fresh thyme or 1 teaspoon dried thyme

1   tablespoon nutritional yeast

Directions:

1   Preheat the oven to 375°F and grease an 8-inch square baking dish.

2   Slice the peeled potatoes lengthwise to 1/8-inch thickness to create long thin "noodles" (this is done most easily with a mandolin slicer). If desired, trim the long edges with a fluted pastry wheel to make them look realistic. Set noodles aside.

3   In a large skillet, heat 2 tablespoons of the avocado oil over medium-high heat. Add the turkey and 1/2 teaspoon of the salt. Brown for 7 to 9 minutes until cooked through, stirring occasionally. Remove the browned turkey and set aside.

4   Add the squash, zucchini, garlic, oregano, and thyme to the same hot pan. Season with the remaining 1/2 teaspoon of salt. Sauté for 5 minutes. Remove skillet from the heat and set aside.

5   In a small dish, stir together the remaining 2 tablespoons of avocado oil and the nutritional yeast.

6   Layer one third of the sweet potato "noodles" in the baking dish. Brush them with one third of the nutritional yeast mixture. Top with half of the zucchini mixture, then half of the meat mixture. Repeat, ending with the noodles. Brush the top layer of noodles with the remaining nutritional yeast mixture. Season with salt to taste.

7   Cover the lasagna with aluminum foil and bake for 35 minutes. Uncover, raise the temperature to 450°F, and bake for an additional 15 minutes, until the top is golden brown, and a toothpick inserted into the center slides easily through the sweet potato noodles. Allow to cool for at least 10 minutes before serving.

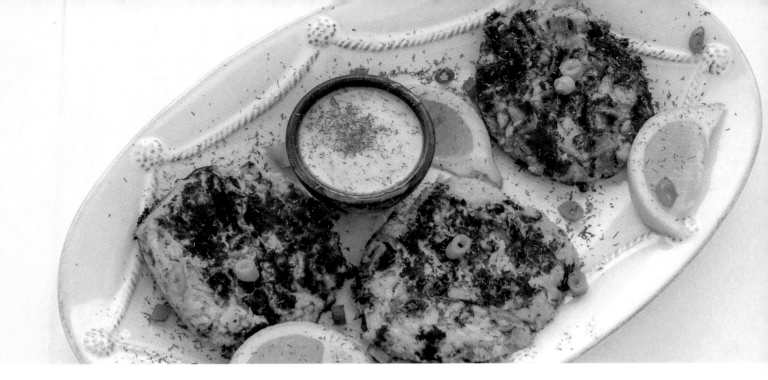

Salmon Croquettes with Dill Aioli

A hit every time I serve it, this classic entrée comes together very quickly with canned salmon. Make sure to serve your croquettes with rich and creamy Dill Aioli (page 35). This simple and nutrient-rich entrée will surely become a staple!

🍴 Prep Time: 10 minutes　　🕐 Cooking Time: 10 minutes　　🎁 Yield: 3-4 servings

Ingredients:

- 2　(6-ounce) cans wild Alaskan boneless salmon, drained
- 1　cup cooked and mashed sweet potatoes or kabocha squash
- 1/4　cup chopped green onions
- 1　tablespoon lemon juice
- 1/2　teaspoon garlic powder
- 3/4　teaspoon sea salt
- 2　tablespoons avocado oil or other heat-stable cooking oil
- 1　recipe Dill Aioli (page 35)
   lemon wedges for garnish

Directions:

1　In a medium bowl, stir together the salmon, sweet potatoes or squash, green onions, lemon juice, garlic powder, and salt. Using 1/3 cup at a time, form six tightly packed patties.

2　Heat the oil in a large skillet over medium-high heat.

3　Fry the patties for 2 to 3 minutes on each side until browned (Flip carefully; with no egg to bind them, they can be fragile. If necessary, reshape the patties with spatula after flipping.). Serve hot with Dill Aioli and lemon wedges.

Baked Tilapia over Greens

30-Minute Meal

If you haven't noticed, my favorite dinners are simple, bursting with flavor, and have an impressive presentation. This dish is just that: perfect for a busy weeknight, yet nice enough to serve to dinner guests. Feel free to add a side of Roasted Sweet Potatoes (page 86) for a more filling meal.

🍴 Prep Time: 10 minutes ⏰ Cooking Time: 20 minutes 🎁 Yield: 4 servings

---

Ingredients:

1	pound baby spinach and/or baby kale greens
3	tablespoons avocado oil or other heat-stable cooking oil
1/4	teaspoon garlic powder, and an additional 1/2 teaspoon for seasoning the filets
4	tilapia filets
2	lemons, sliced, and an additional lemon halved
1	teaspoon sea salt
1	tablespoon capers

Directions:

1 Preheat the oven to 425°F.

2 In a 9 by 13-inch baking dish, toss the greens with the oil and 1/4 teaspoon of the garlic powder.

3 Lay the tilapia filets over the greens. Squeeze the juice of the halved lemon over the filets.

4 Sprinkle the filets with salt and the remaining 1/2 teaspoon garlic. Top each filet with two to three lemon slices. Sprinkle the capers evenly over the filets.

5 Bake for 14 to 18 minutes, until the fish is opaque and flaky and the greens are wilted throughout.

Slow-Cooker Baby Back Ribs

You're going to have to be careful lifting these from your slow cooker, because they will quite literally fall right off the bone! Meals don't come much easier than this, and they also don't come much more delicious. Prepare this recipe in the morning and turn it on low. It will be ready and waiting for you at dinnertime!

Prep Time: 5 minutes   Cooking Time: 7-9 hours

Yield: 4 servings

Ingredients:

1   (3-pound) rack baby back ribs, rinsed and patted dry

1/4   cup maple syrup

1   teaspoon smoked sea salt

1/2   teaspoon garlic powder

1/2   teaspoon dried parsley

1/2   teaspoon onion powder

1/4   teaspoon dried oregano

1/8   teaspoon mace

Directions:

1   Place the ribs in a slow cooker. Brush them with the maple syrup.

2   In a small dish, combine the remaining ingredients. Sprinkle evenly over the ribs, rubbing in as needed.

3   Cook on low for 7 to 9 hours until very tender.

4   Spoon the drippings from the bottom of the slow cooker over ribs before serving.

Lemon–Dill Salmon with Roasted Asparagus

Lemon, dill, and fish always go together so deliciously. This meal is quick, simple, and uses only two pans. In addition, it provides essential nutrients, fatty acids, and crave-worthy flavors! Add a side of Roasted Sweet Potatoes (page 86) for a more filling meal.

Prep Time: 10 minutes   Cooking Time: 10 minutes   Yield: 4 servings

---

Ingredients:

For the salmon:

4   (8-ounce) salmon filets

1   tablespoon avocado oil

1   tablespoon lemon juice

1   teaspoon dried dill

     sea salt

For the asparagus:

1   pound fresh asparagus, trimmed

2   tablespoons avocado oil

     sea salt

Directions:

1   Preheat the oven to 425°F, positioning one rack in the third of the oven closest to the heat source. Grease or line two baking sheets with parchment paper.

2   Arrange the salmon fillets on one baking sheet. Drizzle the salmon with the oil and lemon juice. Sprinkle evenly with the dill and season with the salt to taste. Set aside.

3   Arrange the asparagus in a single layer on the second baking sheet. Pour the oil over the asparagus and toss to evenly coat. Salt to taste.

4   Place both baking sheets on the same rack for 10 minutes, until the salmon flakes easily and the asparagus is fork tender.

Asian Shrimp Bowl

 Full of vegetables and protein, this dish adds an Asian flavor to a nutritious meal.

🍴 Prep Time: 15 minutes   ⏰ Cooking Time: 15 minutes   🎁 Yield: 4 servings

Ingredients:

1	tablespoon avocado oil
1/2	medium yellow onion, diced
3	cloves garlic, minced
3	large carrots, sliced
1/4	cup coconut aminos
3	tablespoons chopped fresh basil or 1 tablespoon dried basil
2	teaspoons fish sauce
1	pound shrimp, peeled and deveined
3	cups fresh baby spinach, loosely packed
6	zucchini spiral cut or julienne cut into noodles

Directions:

1. Heat the oil in a large skillet over medium-high heat. Sauté the onion, garlic, and carrots for 3 to 5 minutes, until the onions are tender.

2. Stir in the coconut aminos, basil, and fish sauce. Add the shrimp and stir-fry until the shrimp are pink and opaque, about 3 minutes.

3. Add the baby spinach to the skillet, cover, and cook until spinach is wilted, about 3 minutes. Toss to combine.

4. In a covered dish, microwave the zucchini noodles for two minutes. Toss them with the shrimp mixture and serve immediately.

Red Wine and Shallot Bison Burgers

Bison is a great source of protein and a great way to expand your meat options. The combination of flavors in this burger is truly satisfying. We love it slathered with Creamy Egg-Free Mayo (page 35) in a lettuce wrap.

 Prep Time: 5 minutes   Cooking Time: 10 minutes

Yield: 4 servings

Ingredients:

1	pound ground bison
2	tablespoons avocado oil
1/3	cup shallots, coarsely chopped
1/3	cup dry red wine
2	tablespoons honey
3	cloves garlic, minced
1/2	teaspoon dried thyme
1/2	teaspoon sea salt

Directions:

1 Heat the grill to medium-high.

2 Mix all the ingredients together and form 4 (1/2 inch thick) patties.

3 Grill the patties for 5 to 7 minutes on each side, until the internal temperature reaches 160°F.

Pan-Fried Round Steak with Rosemary-Roasted Sweet Potatoes

30-Minute Meal

Simple to prepare, full of flavor, and quick to make, this recipe makes the perfect weeknight meal!

🍴 Prep Time: 10 minutes   ⏰ Cooking Time: 20 minutes   🦋 Yield: 4 servings

---

Ingredients:

For the sweet potatoes:

1 1/2	pounds sweet potatoes, chopped into 1-inch pieces
1	medium yellow onion, coarsely chopped
1	teaspoon dried or fresh rosemary
3	tablespoons avocado oil
1/4	teaspoon sea salt

For the steaks:

2	tablespoons avocado oil
1 1/2	pounds tenderized round steaks
1	teaspoon dried parsley
1	teaspoon garlic powder
1	teaspoon sea salt

Directions:

1   Preheat the oven to 425°F, and arrange the oven rack to the third of the oven closest to the heat source. Line a baking sheet with parchment paper.

2   Place the sweet potatoes, onions, and rosemary onto the baking sheet. Pour the avocado oil on top and toss to coat, then season with the salt. Bake for 20 minutes until fork tender.

3   While the potatoes are roasting, prepare the round steaks. Heat the avocado oil in a large skillet over medium heat. Season the steaks with parsley, garlic powder, and salt. Pan fry for 3 to 5 minutes on each side until desired doneness is achieved.

Ground Beef Taco Filling

Creating taco meat that is versatile enough to use in tacos, enchiladas, and salads was important to me. This recipe mimics a more authentic version than a store-bought seasoning packet and is nicely flavored, even without nightshades.

Prep Time: 5 minutes   Cooking Time: 20 minutes

Yield: 4-6 servings

Ingredients:

2	tablespoons avocado oil
1	medium white onion, diced
1	pound ground beef
1	teaspoon dried cilantro or 1 tablespoon fresh cilantro
3/4	teaspoon sea salt
1/2	teaspoon garlic powder

Directions:

1 In a large skillet over medium heat, heat the oil. Add the onions and sauté until translucent, about 5 to 7 minutes.

2 Crumble the ground beef over the onions, sprinkling the seasonings on top.

3 Sauté for 15 minutes, stirring occasionally, until all the meat is browned and cooked throughout.

Slow-Cooker Beef Stroganoff

This hearty dish can be served over Cheesy Cauliflower Rice (page 83), Mashed Fauxtatoes (page 85), or spaghetti squash noodles. This is a warm and comforting meal for those days when you're missing foods from your past.

🍴 Prep Time: 10 minutes   ⏰ Cooking Time: 4-8 hours

👥 Yield: 4 servings

Ingredients:

2	tablespoons avocado oil
1	large yellow onion, halved
1	pound stew beef
1	teaspoon dried parsley
3/4	teaspoon sea salt
1	cup sliced mushrooms, divided
1	cup coconut milk
2	tablespoons nutritional yeast
1	clove garlic, peeled
2	tablespoons arrowroot flour

Directions:

1 Coat the bottom of a slow cooker with avocado oil.

2 Chop one of the onion halves and sprinkle evenly onto the bottom of the slow cooker. Cut the remaining half into chunks and place them in a blender.

3 Place the stew beef in a single layer over the onion. Sprinkle the beef with parsley and salt. Add 1/3 cup of the mushrooms over the beef.

4 Blend the remaining 2/3 cup mushrooms, coconut milk, nutritional yeast, garlic, and arrowroot flour in the blender with the onion half. Pour the mixture over the seasoned beef and mushrooms.

5 Cook on low for 6 to 8 hours or high for 4 hours. Serve over cauliflower rice, zucchini noodles or spaghetti squash.

Easy Slow-Cooker Pot Roast

Meals don't come together much more easily than this roast. Prepare it in the morning or whip it up the night before and refrigerate it overnight. Either way, the flavors and fragrances of this dish will be ready in time for dinner.

Prep Time: 10 minutes   Cooking Time: 6-10 hours   Yield: 4-6 servings

Ingredients:

1	large yellow onion, coarsely chopped
5	large carrots, cut into 2-inch pieces
2	medium sweet potatoes, cut into 1-inch pieces (optional)
3-4	pound chuck roast
2	teaspoons apple cider vinegar
1	teaspoon sea salt
1	teaspoon dried parsley
1	teaspoon dried chives
1/2	teaspoon dried dill
1/2	teaspoon garlic powder
1/4	teaspoon onion powder

Directions:

1. In the order listed, place the onion, carrots, and potatoes into a slow cooker. Rub the roast with vinegar and season with remaining ingredients. Place the roast on top of the vegetables in the slow cooker.

2. Cook on high for 6 to 8 hours or on low for 8 to 10 hours. If omitting the sweet potatoes, serve over Cheesy Cauliflower Rice (page 83) or Mashed Fauxtatoes (page 85).

Peach-Braised Short Ribs

The perfect combination of salty, tangy and sweet, these tender short ribs are sure to become a family favorite!

Prep Time: 5 minutes	Cooking Time: 8 hours	Yield: 4 servings

Ingredients:

1   tablespoon avocado oil

4   pounds beef short ribs

1   (10-ounce) package frozen peaches (about 3 cups)

1   cup Bone Broth (page 19)

1/3   cup honey

1   medium yellow onion, coarsely chopped

2   tablespoons apple cider vinegar

1   tablespoon chopped fresh oregano or 1 teaspoon dried oregano

3   cloves garlic, minced

1   teaspoon smoked sea salt

Directions:

1   Grease the bottom of a slow cooker with the oil. Place the short ribs inside and top with half the peaches.

2   Place the remaining peaches and all other ingredients into a blender. Blend until liquefied and pour over the ribs and peaches.

3   Cook on low for 8 hours. Serve with the peaches and sauce spooned over the top, or continue to the next step.

4   Carefully remove the short ribs from the slow cooker and arrange on a broiler-proof baking sheet. Spoon the peaches and sauce over the ribs and broil for 4 to 6 minutes until browned and bubbly.

Liver & Onions

30-Minute Meal

While I haven't yet been able to convince my husband to try liver, my kids and I really love the way it tastes. In case you're leery, liver is so nutritious that it's known as "nature's multivitamin," and has been prized as a healing food for generations. Organ meat is extremely helpful in autoimmune recovery.

Prep Time: 5 minutes   Cooking Time: 25 minutes   Yield: 4 servings

Ingredients:

2   tablespoons avocado oil

1   large yellow onion, sliced and separated into rings

1   pound beef liver, patted dry

1/2   teaspoon garlic powder

    sea salt

Directions:

1   Heat the oil in a large skillet over medium heat.

2   Sauté the onion rings for 15 minutes until translucent and slightly browned. Stir occasionally.

3   Meanwhile, season the liver with the garlic powder and salt.

4   When the onions are done, remove them from the pan and set aside.

5   Arrange the liver pieces in the skillet. Cook for 4 to 5 minutes on each side.

6   When the liver is finished cooking, return the onions to the pan. Cook for 2 to 3 more minutes.

Thrown-Together Meatballs

These lovely meatballs are perfect on top of a bed of zucchini noodles or as an appetizer served with I Can't Believe It's Nomato Sauce (page 114)!

🍴 Prep Time: 5 minutes　　　⏰ Cooking Time: 20 minutes　　　👥 Yield: 4-6 servings

---

Ingredients:

1	pound ground beef
1	tablespoon coconut flour
1/2	cup Bone Broth (page 19)
1	teaspoon dried basil
1	teaspoon dried oregano
1	teaspoon dried parsley
1/2	teaspoon garlic powder
1/2	teaspoon onion powder
1/2	teaspoon dried thyme
1/2	teaspoon sea salt

Directions:

1 Preheat the oven to 350°F. Grease or line a baking sheet with parchment paper.

2 Mix all the ingredients together. Divide the mixture into 12 (1 1/2-inch) balls, arrange on the baking sheet, and bake for 20 minutes.

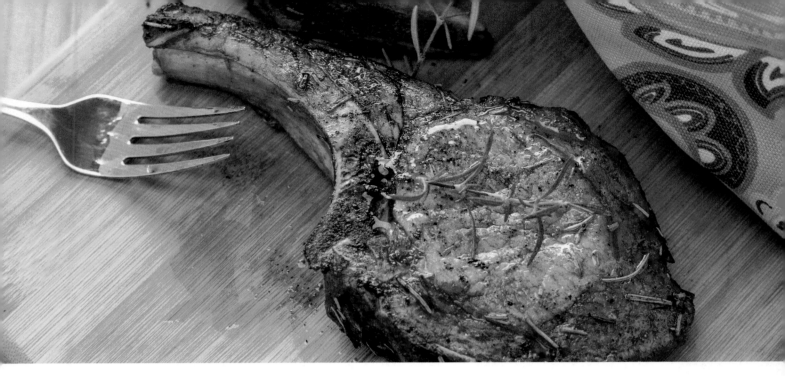

Balsamic Pork Chops

These chops are slightly sweet, salty, and have a touch of Balsamic tang! Marinate them all day and toss them on the grill just in time for dinner.

🍴 Prep Time: 5 minutes   ⏰ Marinate Time: 3-12 hours   ⏰ Cooking Time: 15 minutes   🎁 Yield: 4 servings

Ingredients:

4   thick-cut pork chops

3   tablespoons Balsamic vinegar

2   tablespoons pure maple syrup

1   tablespoon fresh rosemary or 1 teaspoon dried rosemary

1/4   teaspoon garlic powder

    sea salt

Directions:

1   In a sealed container in the refrigerator, marinate the pork in all the other ingredients for 3 to 12 hours.

2   To grill, sear each side for 2 minutes over medium-high heat, then reduce the heat to low and cook for 15 more minutes until slightly firm to the touch and the internal temperature reaches 145°F degrees. Remove from the grill, cover with aluminum foil, and let stand for 5 minutes before serving.

Honey-Seared Pork Tenderloin

An absolute crowd-pleaser, I've never served this entrée without 100 percent rave reviews. This tenderloin is quick and easy to prepare, and with all the ingredients stored easily in your freezer or pantry, what more could you want?

Prep Time: 10 minutes   Cooking Time: 25 minutes   Yield: 4 servings

Ingredients:

1 1/2	pound whole pork tenderloin
1/4	teaspoon sea salt
1/4	teaspoon garlic powder
1/4	teaspoon onion powder
1/8	teaspoon dried oregano
1/8	teaspoon dried thyme
1/8	teaspoon ground cloves
2	tablespoons honey
1/4	cup coconut oil

Directions:

1. Preheat the oven to 375°F.

2. In a small bowl, mix the herbs and seasonings together. Rub them into the pork tenderloin, and set the tenderloin aside.

3. In a large oven-proof skillet or pot, stir the honey and coconut oil over medium heat until melted.

4. Brown the tenderloin in the oil mixture for 1-2 minutes on each side.

5. With the tenderloin inside, place the uncovered oven-proof skillet in the oven for 15 to 20 minutes, or until the internal temperature reaches 145°F. Watch carefully to avoid burning the honey mixture. If it begins to turn dark brown, move the skillet down to a lower oven rack Remove the skillet from the oven, cover with aluminum foil, and let sit for 5 minutes before carving.

6. Slice the pork diagonally and drizzle the pan drippings over the top to serve.

I Can't Believe It's Nomato Sauce

Tomatoes are one of my favorite foods. Unfortunately, my tummy doesn't always agree. This tomato-free marinara sauce is a great way to sneak vegetables into a meal. And unlike any "nomato" sauce I've tried, this recipe creates the perfect zest to replace tomato's acidity. The secret is in the addition of lemon juice and capers. The color is also beautifully matched to a traditional tomato sauce, so don't worry, your secret is safe; they won't know it's nomato sauce!

Prep Time: 20 minutes   Cooking Time: 40 minutes   Yield: 4-6 servings

Ingredients:

3	slices bacon
1	medium red beet, cut into 1-inch chunks
1	medium yellow onion, coarsely chopped
4	cloves garlic, peeled and halved
3	large carrots, sliced (about 2 cups)
1 1/4	cup Bone Broth (page 19)
1 1/2	teaspoons sea salt
1/4	cup chopped fresh basil
1	teaspoon dried oregano
2	tablespoons lemon juice
2	teaspoons capers

Directions:

1   Fill a medium saucepan halfway with water and bring it to a boil. Meanwhile, in a large skillet, fry the bacon on medium heat until most of its fat is rendered, about 7 minutes, turning occasionally. When finished, set the bacon aside while reserving the grease in the pan.

2   Add the beet chunks to the boiling water and boil for 10 minutes, or until just fork tender. When finished, drain, discard the water, rinse thoroughly, and set aside.

3   Add the onion and garlic to the hot bacon grease, and sauté for 5 minutes. Meanwhile, tear the cooked bacon into 1-inch pieces. Add the beets, raw carrots, and bacon to the onion mixture and sauté for 5 more minutes.

4   Add the broth, salt, basil, and oregano to the pan; simmer for 10 minutes covered, with the lid partially vented.

5   Carefully pour the entire mixture into a blender or food processor. Add the lemon juice and capers and process until smooth and the color is red throughout. Serve hot over spaghetti squash or zucchini noodles.

Italian Sausage

In pizzas, pastas, or just by itself, Italian sausage adds complexity and flavor to many different entrees. Don't be intimidated by making your own sausage. All you need to do is season ground meat with a few dried spices!

🍴 Prep Time: 5 minutes   ⏰ Cooking Time: 12 minutes

👥 Yield: 1 pound

Ingredients:

1	pound ground pork
1	teaspoon dried basil
1	teaspoon dried oregano
1	teaspoon dried parsley
1/2	teaspoon garlic powder
1/2	teaspoon onion powder
1/2	teaspoon dried thyme
1/2	teaspoon sea salt
2	tablespoons avocado oil

Directions:

1. Mix the meat with the spices until uniformly combined.

2. Heat the oil in a large skillet over medium heat. Crumble the meat into the hot oil and cook for 10 to 12 minutes, stirring frequently, until browned and cooked through.

Variation:

Feel free to mix up the types of meats when preparing this entrée. While pork is a more traditional way to prepare sausage, this recipe can be made with ground beef, lamb, turkey, bison, or any ground meat of your preference.

Desserts &
Beverages

Chocolate Cupcakes

Chocolate flavor, a rounded top, and a beautiful texture throughout—these cupcakes are perfect for a birthday or other special occasion!

🍴 Prep Time: 15 minutes   ⏰ Cooking Time: 35 minutes

🎁 Yield: 12 cupcakes

Ingredients:

2/3	cup coconut flour
1/2	cup arrowroot flour
1/3	cup carob powder
2	teaspoons ground cinnamon
1 1/2	teaspoons cream of tartar
1	teaspoon baking soda
1/2	teaspoon sea salt
1 1/4	cup pumpkin purée
1/3	cup coconut butter, softened
2	teaspoons lemon juice
1/2	cup coconut oil
1/4	cup maple syrup
1 1/2	teaspoon vanilla extract
1	Gelatin Egg Substitute (page 18), prepared when directed
1	recipe Salted Caramel Frosting (page 119)

Directions:

1. Preheat the oven to 350°F and line a 12-cup muffin tin with paper liners.

2. In a small bowl, whisk together the flours, carob, cinnamon, cream of tartar, baking soda, and salt.

3. In a large mixing bowl or stand mixer, cream together the pumpkin purée, coconut butter, lemon juice, coconut oil, maple syrup, and vanilla.

4. Prepare the gelatin egg substitute and add it to the wet mixture. Beat on medium speed to incorporate.

5. Add the dry ingredients, beating on medium speed until combined.

6. Divide and roll the dough into 12 equal balls (about 1/4 cup each), and place one ball into each muffin cup. (Do not push down; the dough will expand to fill the cup as it bakes.)

7. Bake for 35 minutes, until cupcakes are firm to the touch and a toothpick inserted into the center comes out clean. Cool completely on a wire rack.

Chocolate Mousse

Lusciously creamy and decadently chocolaty, this mousse is a perfect topping for any cake, cupcake or alone as a special treat!

⏱ Prep Time: 5 minutes
👥 Yield: 3 cups or 6 servings

Ingredients:

3	large avocados
3/4	cup coconut milk
2/3	cup honey
1/2	cup carob powder
1	teaspoon ground cinnamon
	pinch sea salt

Directions:

Blend all the ingredients in a food processor until completely smooth and creamy. Serve as a pudding dessert, or spread onto cake, brownies, or cookies. This keeps well for 3 to 4 days in the refrigerator.

Salted Caramel Frosting

Perfectly flavored and beautifully fluffy, this recipe does not seem one bit paleo!

⏱ Prep Time: 15 minutes
⏰ Cooking Time: 5 minutes
👥 Yield: 3 cups frosting

Ingredients:

1/2	cup coconut palm sugar
2	tablespoons water
1 1/2	cups palm shortening
1/2	cup arrowroot flour
1/4	teaspoon sea salt

Directions:

1 In a small saucepan on medium heat, dissolve the sugar into the water. Stir constantly and do not let boil.

2 Pour the dissolved sugar mixture into a mixing bowl. Beat on high for 2 minutes, until cool to the touch. (Don't skip this. If it's not cool, the frosting won't whip.)

3 Add the shortening, flour, and salt. Beat on high for 5 minutes, until whipped and fluffy.

Strawberry Frosting

Delectably light and fluffy, this frosting is simply perfect on a paleo cake!

⏱ Prep Time: 10 minutes
⏰ Cooking Time: 5 minutes
👥 Yield: 3 cups frosting

Ingredients:

1/4	cup water
2/3	cup evaporated cane juice
1/2	cup fresh strawberries, coarsely chopped
1 1/2	cups palm shortening
2/3	cup arrowroot flour

Directions:

1 In a small saucepan on medium heat, dissolve the evaporated cane juice into the water. Stir constantly and do not let boil.

2 Pour the dissolved sugar mixture into a mixing bowl, and add the strawberries. Beat on high for 2 minutes, until cool to the touch. (Don't skip this. If it's not cool, the frosting won't whip.)

3 Add the shortening and flour. Beat on high for 5 minutes, until whipped and fluffy.

Yellow Cake

Not only is this cake beautiful, it's sweet, light, and airy—perfect for any special occasion!

Prep Time: 20 minutes   Cooking Time: 22 minutes

Yield: 16 servings

Ingredients:

2/3	cup coconut flour
2/3	cup arrowroot flour
2	teaspoons cream of tartar
1 1/2	teaspoon baking soda
1	teaspoon salt
2/3	cup unsweetened applesauce
2/3	cup coconut oil, softened
1/3	cup honey
1/4	cup coconut butter, softened
1	tablespoon lemon juice
1	teaspoon vanilla extract
2	Gelatin Egg Substitutes (page 18), prepared when directed
1	recipe Chocolate Mousse (page 119)

Directions:

1   Preheat the oven to 350°F. Line a 12 by 18-inch jelly roll pan with parchment paper.

2   In a small bowl, whisk together the flours, cream of tartar, baking soda, and salt.

3   In a large mixing bowl or stand mixer, cream together the applesauce, oil, honey, coconut butter, lemon juice, and vanilla.

4   Prepare the gelatin egg substitutes and add them to the wet mixture. Mix on medium until completely smooth.

5   Add the dry ingredients to the wet mixture, beating on medium speed until well combined.

6   Spread the batter evenly into the prepared pan. (It will be quite thin.)

7   Bake on the middle rack for 22 minutes.

8   Cool for 5 minutes in the pan, then cool completely on a wire rack before frosting.

9   Cut the cake in half, lengthwise, then cut each half into thirds. If the cake pan is exactly 12 by 18 inches, each square should be 6 inches square. If the pan dimensions are less than 12 by 18 inches, adjust the sizes accordingly.

10   To frost, place a cake layer onto a serving platter. Spread 1/4 cup of the frosting over the top. Repeat until all layers are stacked and frosted. Use the remaining frosting to frost the outside of the cake.

Strawberry Layer Cake

This cake is my go-to dessert. I serve it to non-paleo eaters often, and it is always well-received!

🍴 Prep Time: 20 minutes   ⏰ Cooking Time: 22 minutes

🎁 Yield: 16 servings

Ingredients:

2/3	cup coconut flour
2/3	cup arrowroot flour
2	teaspoons cream of tartar
1 1/2	teaspoons baking soda
1	teaspoon salt
1	cup fresh strawberries, diced, plus an additional 2 cups sliced to add to the frosting
2/3	cup coconut oil, softened
1/3	cup honey
1/4	cup coconut butter, softened
1	tablespoon lemon juice
1	teaspoon vanilla extract
2	Gelatin Egg Substitutes (page 18), prepared when directed
1	recipe Strawberry Frosting (page 119)

Directions:

1. Preheat the oven to 350°F and line a jelly roll pan or a 12 by 18-inch cake pan with parchment paper.

2. In a small bowl, whisk together the flours, cream of tartar, baking soda, and salt.

3. In a food processor, process the diced strawberries, oil, honey, coconut butter, lemon juice, and vanilla until smooth. Set aside.

4. Prepare the gelatin egg substitutes and add them to the wet ingredients in the food processor. Add the dry ingredients and process until completely combined.

5. Spread the batter evenly into the prepared pan. (It will be quite thin.) Bake on the middle rack for 20 to 22 minutes, until the center is slightly firm to the touch.

6. Cool for 5 minutes in the pan, then cool completely on a wire rack before cutting and frosting.

7. Cut cake in half, lengthwise, then cut each half into thirds. If the cake pan is exactly 12 by 18 inches, each square should be 6 inches square. If the pan dimensions are less than 12x18 inches, adjust the sizes accordingly.

8. To frost, place a cake layer onto a serving platter. Spread 1/4 cup of frosting over the top followed by a single layer of sliced strawberries. Repeat until all layers are stacked and frosted. Use the remaining frosting to frost the outside of the cake and garnish with remaining strawberries, if desired.

Carob Brownies

A fudgy cocoa alternative, these egg-free brownies have a fantastic texture. Enjoy them alone or topped with Ultra-Creamy Mint Ice Cream (page 138) for an extra-decadent treat!

Prep Time: 10 minutes   Cooking Time: 12 minutes   Yield: 12 servings

Ingredients:

1/4	cup coconut flour
1/3	cup carob powder
2	tablespoons coconut palm sugar
3/4	teaspoon baking soda
1	teaspoon cream of tartar
1	teaspoon sea salt
1/2	teaspoon ground cinnamon
1/2	cup pitted dates, gently packed
1/4	cup coconut oil
1	teaspoon vanilla extract
2	tablespoons coconut butter
2	tablespoons coconut milk
1 1/2	teaspoon lemon juice
1	Gelatin Egg Substitute (page 18), prepared when directed

Directions:

1   Preheat the oven to 350°F and grease an 8-inch square baking dish.

2   In a small bowl, whisk the flour, carob, sugar, baking soda, cream of tartar, salt, and cinnamon. Set aside. Place the dates, oil, vanilla, coconut butter, milk and lemon juice in a food processor. Process until very smooth.

3   Prepare the gelatin egg substitute and add it to the food processor. Process to combine. Add the flour mixture as well and process the dough until smooth.

4   Spread the dough into the prepared pan. Bake for 12 to 14 minutes, until a toothpick inserted in the center comes out clean and the brownies are slightly firm to the touch.

Blackberry Cobbler

This dessert is incredibly simple, but it makes a delicious and beautiful dish you can proudly bring to a party or picnic! Serve alone or with a scoop of coconut cream on top.

Prep Time: 10 minutes   Cooking Time: 35 minutes   Yield: 8 servings

Ingredients:

1	(12-ounce) package fresh blackberries
2	tablespoons coconut oil, softened, plus additional for greasing the baking dish
3	tablespoons water
1/4	cup arrowroot flour
1/4	cup coconut flour
1/4	cup honey
1/4	teaspoon salt
3/4	teaspoon baking soda
1 1/2	teaspoons lemon juice

Directions:

1. Preheat the oven to 300°F and grease an 8-inch square baking dish.

2. Spread the blackberries evenly in the bottom of the pan.

3. In a medium mixing bowl or stand mixer, mix the remaining ingredients with a whisk or on medium speed until combined. Spread over the blackberries.

4. Bake for 35 to 40 minutes, until the entire top is golden brown.

Graham Pie Crust

A honey-sweetened graham crust, this is a perfect base for no-bake, custard-style pies!

Prep Time: 15 minutes   Cooking Time: 10 minutes   Yield: One 9-inch pie crust

Ingredients:

1/2	cup coconut flour
2	tablespoons arrowroot flour
3/4	teaspoon ground cinnamon
1/4	teaspoon sea salt
1/4	teaspoon baking soda
1/3	cup coconut oil, melted
1/2	teaspoon vanilla extract
3	tablespoons honey
1	Gelatin Egg Substitute (page 18), prepared when directed

Tip:

For a starch-free crust, simply omit the arrowroot flour.

Directions:

1 Preheat oven to 350°F.

2 In small bowl, whisk together the flours, cinnamon, salt, and baking soda. Set aside.

3 In a large mixing bowl or stand mixer, mix the oil, vanilla, and honey on medium speed until combined.

4 Prepare the gelatin egg substitute and add it to the wet mixture. Beat on medium speed to incorporate.

5 Add the dry ingredients to the wet ingredients. Mix on medium-low speed until fully combined.

6 Scrape the batter into a pie plate. Grease your fingertips with oil and spread the dough into the pie plate and up the sides. (Do this step immediately after the dough is combined. The dough will thicken as the gelatin sets and become less pliable.) Mold dough as needed to completely cover bottom and sides of pie plate.

7 Bake for 10 to 12 minutes, until golden brown.

Pastry Crust

I originally called this recipe the "million-dollar pie crust," because that's about how much I spent on ingredients trying to get a crust that could hold up! All joking aside, though, this is a delicious crust that can be baked before filling or baked with the filling inside.

Prep Time: 15 minutes   Cooking Time: 15 minutes   Yield: One 9-inch pie crust

Ingredients:

1/2	cup coconut flour
1/4	cup arrowroot flour
1/4	teaspoon sea salt
1	Gelatin Egg Substitute (page 18), prepared when directed
1/3	cup palm shortening or lard
6	tablespoons ice water

Directions:

1 Preheat the oven to 350°F.

2 In a food processor, pulse the flours and salt until combined, about four or five pulses.

3 Prepare the gelatin egg and add it to the food processor. Pulse five or six more times, until crumbly.

4 Add the shortening or lard to the food processor. Pulse five or six more times.

5 Add the water 1 tablespoon at a time. Pulse two or three times after each addition to combine. (The mixture will be slightly crumbly.)

6 Pour the dough directly into a pie plate. Press into the bottom and sides, fluting the edges if desired.

7 Use in your recipe as directed or, for a prebaked crust, bake for 15 to 17 minutes.

Dutch Apple Pie

I wasn't even out of elementary school when Miss Sheri taught me to make an apple pie. Sheri's family had an apple orchard and could bake and cook with the best of them. I'll never forget learning to make her famous Dutch apple pie in her old farmhouse. As you can imagine, this was a special recipe for me to adapt to the AIP diet.

Prep Time: 30 minutes   Cooking Time: 1 hour

Yield: 8 servings

Ingredients:

For the Pie Crust:

Pie Crust, unbaked (page 125)

For the filling:

3   tablespoons evaporated cane juice

1   teaspoon cinnamon

5-6   medium Granny Smith apples, peeled, cored, and sliced

For the crumb topping:

1/2   cup shredded unsweetened coconut

1   teaspoon ground cinnamon

3   tablespoons evaporated cane juice

1/4   cup coconut oil

Directions:

1   Preheat the oven to 350°F.

2   In a small dish, mix the evaporated cane juice and cinnamon. Set aside.

3   Layer half of the apples in the unbaked pie crust. Sprinkle half of the cinnamon mixture over the apples. Repeat with the remaining apples and cinnamon mixture.

4   To prepare the crumb topping, mix all of the ingredients together until uniformly combined and moistened throughout. Crumble over the apples.

5   Bake, uncovered, for 20 minutes. Open the oven and tent the pie loosely with aluminum foil to avoid over-browning. Bake for an additional 30-40 minutes, until golden brown on top and apples are tender but not mushy.

Coconut Cream Pie

Paleo and non-paleo alike, this recipe is hands down my husband's favorite dessert. I love this pie because I can take it to get-togethers without a single person ever guessing it's a paleo or allergen-free version.

🍴 Prep Time: 15 minutes	⏰ Cooking Time: 5 minutes
🌡 Chilling Time: 4 hours	🎁 Yield: 8 servings

Ingredients:

1	Graham Pie Crust, baked and cooled (page 124)
1	cup shredded, unsweetened coconut, plus an additional 1/4 cup for garnish (optional)
2	(13.5-ounce) cans coconut milk
1/2	cup arrowroot flour
1/3	cup honey
1 1/2	teaspoons vanilla
1/4	teaspoon sea salt
	coconut whipped topping (optional)

Directions:

1. Preheat the oven to 350°F.

2. In a single layer on a baking sheet, toast the coconut for 5 to 7 minutes, until it is golden brown (Do not skip this step; without it, the pie will be colorless and semi-translucent. The toasting also adds great flavor!)

3. In a medium saucepan over medium-high heat, whisk all the ingredients together except for the toasted coconut.

4. Bring the mixture to a boil, uncovered, stirring frequently while scraping the bottom and sides. Boil for 1 minute. (Mixture will thicken significantly.)

5. Stir in the coconut (reserving the additional 1/4 cup of coconut for the optional garnish) and pour the mixture into the prepared pie crust.

6. Refrigerate for 4 hours, until completely cool and solidified. Garnish with toasted coconut.

Key Lime Pie

Key lime pie is perfect for a springtime or summertime treat! The creaminess comes from the avocado, but don't worry, you won't taste it one bit!

🍴 Prep Time: 5 minutes   🌡 Chilling Time: 4 hours   🎁 Yield: 8 servings

---

Ingredients:

1   Graham Pie Crust, baked and cooled (page 124)

1   (13.5-ounce) can coconut milk

2/3 cup key lime juice, freshly squeezed

3/4 cup honey

1/4 teaspoon sea salt

3/4 cup mashed avocado

1   Gelatin Egg Substitute (page 18), prepared when directed

Directions:

1   In a blender, blend the milk, lime juice, honey, salt, and avocado until very creamy.

2   Prepare the gelatin egg and add it to the blender. Blend until completely smooth. Pour the mixture into the cooled pie crust and refrigerate for 4 hours, or until set and solidified. Serve cold with coconut whipped cream, if desired.

Tips:

Note: Since this is a no-bake filling, the gelatin egg substitute in this recipe cannot be replaced with an egg. Once refrigerated, the gelatin in this filling will solidify the filling into a custard.

Pumpkin Pie Bars

*Pumpkin pie has always been a favorite of mine.
I absolutely love it any time of year! Serve this
by itself or topped with coconut cream.*

🍴 Prep Time: 20 minutes	⏰ Cooking Time: 15 minutes
🌡 Chilling Time: 4 hours	🎁 Yield: 12 servings

Ingredients:

For the crust:

1/2 cup coconut flour
1/4 teaspoon sea salt
1/3 cup coconut oil or palm shortening
2 Gelatin Egg Substitutes (page 18), prepared when directed

For the filling:

1 (13.5-ounce) can pumpkin puree
1/2 cup honey
1/2 cup coconut butter, softened
1 teaspoon ground cinnamon
1/2 teaspoon ground ginger
1/8 teaspoon ground cloves
1/8 teaspoon ground mace

Directions:

1 Preheat the oven to 350°F.

2 **For the crust:** In a medium mixing bowl, whisk the flour and salt. Add the oil and stir to combine.

3 Prepare the gelatin egg substitutes and add them to the flour mixture. Stir until completely incorporated. Press the dough into an 8-inch square baking dish. (Placing parchment paper over the dough makes pressing it mess-free and simple.) Bake for 15 to 17 minutes, until the edges are golden brown and the center is firm to the touch. Set the baking dish on a wire rack to cool completely.

4 **For the filing:** In a medium mixing bowl, cream all of the filling ingredients together on medium speed or with a whisk. Spread evenly into the cooled crust.

5 Refrigerate for 4 hours, until set and firm to the touch.

Tips:

Sometimes for a quick and easy treat, I make "pumpkin fudge" by preparing these without the crust. Simply spread the filling into a baking dish and cut it into squares once it's chilled.

N'oatmeal Crème Pies

This was my first "viral" recipe, and it put my blog on the map. It has been shared and enjoyed by thousands of people, and I hope you'll see why! If you've ever enjoyed a packaged "oatmeal crème pie," you'll fall in love with this nutrient-packed, allergen-free version!

🍴 Prep Time: 30 minutes   ⏰ Cooking Time: 21 minutes   👥 Yield: 16 cookie pies

Ingredients:

For the cookies:

1/3	cup coconut flour
2	teaspoons ground cinnamon
1	teaspoon baking soda
1/2	teaspoon sea salt
1	cup mashed sweet potato or pumpkin puree
1/2	cup pitted dates, gently packed
1/4	cup coconut oil
1	teaspoon vanilla extract
1 1/2	teaspoon lemon juice
1	Gelatin Egg Substitute (page 18), prepared when directed
1/2	cup shredded unsweetened coconut

For the filling:

3	tablespoons water, with an additional 3 tablespoons for the honey mixture.
1	tablespoon gelatin
1/3	cup honey
	pinch of sea salt

Directions:

1. Preheat the oven to 350°F. Grease or line two baking sheets with parchment paper.

2. In a small bowl, mix together the flour, cinnamon, baking soda, and salt. Set aside.

3. In a food processor, process the sweet potato, dates, oil, vanilla, and lemon juice until smooth.

4. Prepare the gelatin egg substitute and add it, along with the dry ingredients, to the food processor and process again until the dough is smooth.

5. Add the coconut and pulse to incorporate.

6. Spacing them evenly, drop tablespoonfuls of cookie dough onto each prepared cookie sheet. With a small piece of parchment paper, gently press each cookie into 1 1/2-inch circles of about 1/4-inch thickness.

7. Bake for 16 minutes, until the cookies are slightly firm to the touch. Cool on a wire rack.

8. **For the filling:** While the cookies are cooling, prepare the filling. In a stand mixer or a large mixing bowl, whisk together 3 tablespoons of water with the gelatin. Set aside.

9. In a small saucepan over medium heat, whisk together the remaining 3 tablespoons of water, honey, and salt. Bring to a boil and boil for exactly 5 minutes.

10. Carefully transfer the boiling honey mixture into the mixing bowl, pouring over the rubbery gelatin. Begin to mix slowly, gradually increasing the speed to high to avoid splattering the hot liquid. Beat on high for 2-5 minutes, until the mixture becomes a thick, marshmallow-like crème.

11. Right after the crème is finished whipping, use a regular dining spoon to spoon dollops of crème onto the back of one cooled cookie. Pick up another cookie and gently press them together back-to-back to squish the crème filling to the edges. Repeat with all the cookies.

Desserts & Beverages

131

Pumpkin Spice Macaroons

As simple as can be, these fall-flavored macaroons will satisfy your sweet tooth and supply you with loads of nutrition and fiber!

Prep Time: 10 minutes   Cooking Time: 15 minutes   Yield: 30 cookies

Ingredients:

2   cups shredded unsweetened coconut

1   cup firmly packed pitted dates

2/3   cup pumpkin puree

2   tablespoons honey

1   teaspoon ground cinnamon

1/2   teaspoon ground ginger

1/4   teaspoon ground cloves

1/8   teaspoon ground mace

Directions:

1   Preheat the oven to 350°F, and grease or line two baking sheets with parchment paper.

2   Process all the ingredients in a food processor until the mixture is smooth.

3   Scoop out balls of dough by the tablespoonful and arrange them evenly on the baking sheets. Press each one down to form 1/2-inch-thick discs.

4   Bake for 13 to 15 minutes, until the bottoms are browned. Cool completely on a wire rack.

Snickerdoodles

Snickerdoodles have always been a favorite of mine, and a grain-free, egg-free, and dairy-free version is exactly what I needed to fill the void. These are soft, airy, and delicious! For a firmer cookie, store these in the refrigerator.

🍴 Prep Time: 15 minutes   ⏰ Cooking Time: 14 minutes

🎁 Yield: 18 cookies

Ingredients:

For the cookies:

1/3	cup coconut flour
1/3	cup arrowroot flour
1	teaspoon cream of tartar
1/2	teaspoon baking soda
1/4	teaspoon sea salt
1/3	cup unsweetened applesauce, at room temperature
1/4	cup coconut butter, softened
1 1/2	teaspoons lemon juice
2	tablespoons honey
2	tablespoons coconut oil
1	teaspoon vanilla extract
1	Gelatin Egg Substitute (page 18), prepared when directed

For the cinnamon-sugar coating:

1	teaspoon ground cinnamon
2	tablespoons evaporated cane juice

Directions:

1 Preheat the oven to 350°F and line two baking sheets with parchment paper.

2 In a small bowl, whisk together the flours, cream of tartar, baking soda, and salt.

3 In a large mixing bowl or stand mixer, cream together the applesauce, coconut butter, lemon juice, honey, oil, and vanilla.

4 Prepare the gelatin egg substitute and add it to the wet mixture. Mix on medium speed to incorporate.

5 Add the dry ingredients to the wet ingredients and mix on medium-low speed until combined. Set aside.

6 In a small bowl, stir together the cinnamon and evaporated cane juice.

7 Scoop 1 tablespoon of dough out at a time to form 18 balls. Roll each in the cinnamon mixture, coating it on all sides.

8 Arrange the cookies on the baking sheets. With the bottom of a drinking glass, flatten the balls into 1/2-inch-thick discs.

9 Bake for 14 minutes, until the bottoms are golden brown and firm to the touch. Cool completely on a wire rack.

Frosted Lemon Cookies

I never cared for lemon desserts until I was pregnant with our first child, Daniel. I craved lemony sweets the whole time and never lost my taste for them. These little cookies are sweet, sour, and perfect for a treat!

🍴 Prep Time: 20 minutes   ⏰ Cooking Time: 14 minutes

🎁 Yield: 18 cookies

Ingredients:

For the cookies:

1/3	cup coconut flour
1/3	cup arrowroot flour
1	teaspoon cream of tartar
1/2	teaspoon baking soda
1/4	teaspoon sea salt
1/8	teaspoon ground turmeric
1/3	cup unsweetened applesauce, at room temperature
1/4	cup coconut butter, softened
2	tablespoons palm shortening
2	tablespoons honey
1 1/2	teaspoons lemon juice
1	tablespoon grated lemon zest
1	teaspoon vanilla extract
1	Gelatin Egg Substitute (page 18), prepared when directed

For the frosting:

2	tablespoons coconut butter
2	tablespoons palm shortening
2	tablespoons honey
2	tablespoons lemon juice
1	tablespoon lemon zest, freshly grated

Directions:

1   Preheat the oven to 350°F and line two baking sheets with parchment paper.

2   In a small mixing bowl, whisk together the flours, cream of tartar, baking soda, salt, and turmeric.

3   In a large mixing bowl or stand mixer, cream together the applesauce, coconut butter, shortening, honey, lemon juice, lemon zest, and vanilla.

4   Prepare the gelatin egg substitute and add it to the wet mixture. Mix on medium speed to incorporate.

5   Add the dry ingredients to the wet ingredients and mix on medium-low speed until combined. Set aside.

6   Scoop 1 tablespoon of dough out at a time and form balls. Arrange the cookies on the baking sheets. With the bottom of a drinking glass, flatten the balls into 1/2-inch-thick discs.

7   Bake for 14 minutes, until the bottom of the cookies are golden and the centers are firm to the touch. Cool on a wire rack.

8   Prepare the frosting: Mix together the coconut butter, shortening, honey, and lemon juice until completely smooth and free from lumps. Spread the frosting evenly over the cooled cookies, garnishing with the lemon zest.

Carob Crinkles

I've made the traditional wheat-flour version of this cookie for years. I grew up on them as a child, and now their allergen-free version is my husband's favorite post-dinner cookie, too!

🍴 Prep Time: 15 minutes	⏰ Cooking Time: 16 minutes	🎁 Yield: 18 cookies

Ingredients:

For the dusting:

3	tablespoons evaporated cane juice
1	tablespoon arrowroot flour

For the cookies:

1/4	cup coconut flour
1/4	cup arrowroot flour
3	tablespoons carob powder
3/4	teaspoon cream of tartar
3/4	teaspoon baking soda
1	teaspoon ground cinnamon
1/4	teaspoon sea salt
1/3	cup pumpkin purée
1/3	cup maple syrup
3	tablespoons coconut butter, softened
2	tablespoons palm shortening
1 1/2	teaspoons lemon juice
1	teaspoon vanilla extract
1	Gelatin Egg Substitute (page 18), prepared when directed

Directions:

1 Preheat the oven to 350°F and line two baking sheets with parchment paper.

2 Place the dusting ingredients in a high-speed blender and blend on high for 1 minute. Let the powder settle before opening the lid. Transfer to a small mixing bowl and set aside until step 7.

3 In a small mixing bowl, whisk together the flours, carob, cream of tartar, baking soda, cinnamon, and salt.

4 In a large mixing bowl or stand mixer, cream together the pumpkin, maple syrup, coconut butter, shortening, lemon juice, and vanilla.

5 Prepare the gelatin egg substitute and add it to the wet mixture. Mix on medium speed to incorporate.

6 Add the dry ingredients to the wet ingredients and beat on medium speed until combined.

7 Scoop 1 tablespoon of dough out at a time and form balls. Roll each ball in the dusting mixture, coating all sides. Arrange on the baking sheets and press down with the bottom of a drinking glass until the balls are 1/2-inch-thick discs.

8 Bake for 16 minutes, until the cookies are firm to the touch.

Gingerbread Cookies

These cookies are a breeze to whip up and are perfect as cut-out cookies, gingerbread houses, or gingersnaps!

🍴 Prep Time: 20 minutes   ⏰ Cooking Time: 17-21 minutes   🎁 Yield: 18 cookies or gingersnaps, or 1 Gingerbread House + a few extra cookies

Ingredients:

For the Gingerbread:

1	cup coconut flour
1 1/2	teaspoon ground ginger
1	teaspoon ground cinnamon
1/2	teaspoon sea salt
1/2	teaspoon baking soda
1/2	cup palm shortening or coconut oil, softened
1/2	cup honey
1/4	cup blackstrap molasses
1 1/2	teaspoons vanilla extract
2	Gelatin Egg Substitutes (page 18), prepared when directed

For the frosting:

1	cup palm shortening
3/4	cup honey

For the décor:

Dried fruits such as: blueberries, apricots. bananas, cranberries, (look for organic varieties that use evaporated cane juice instead of refined sugar)
Unsweetened shredded coconut

Directions:

1. Preheat the oven to 350°F and line two baking sheets with parchment paper.

2. In a small bowl, whisk together the flour, ginger, cinnamon, salt, and baking soda.

3. In a large bowl or stand mixer, mix the shortening, honey, molasses, and vanilla on medium speed to combine.

4. Prepare the gelatin egg substitutes and add them to the wet mixture. Mix on medium speed just until the gelatin egg substitutes are incorporated.

5. Add the dry ingredients to the wet ingredients and mix on medium-high speed until thoroughly combined and creamy. Scrape the dough between two large pieces of parchment paper and roll to 1/4-inch thickness.

6. **For gingersnaps:** Score into desired size with a pizza cutter. **For cut-out cookies:** Use cookie cutters to cut out shapes. **For gingerbread house:** Use the pattern on page 146.

7. Bake for 17 to 21 minutes, until cookies reach desired firmness. Cool completely on a wire rack before frosting or building.

8. **For the frosting:** Beat the shortening and honey together on high until whipped and fluffy.

Chocolate Ice Cream

While chocolate may be off-limits in the Autoimmune Protocol, carob is not! This ice cream is perfect for birthdays, special occasions, or just because!

 Prep Time: 10 minutes   Cooking Time: 10 minutes

Chilling Time: 4-8 hours   Yield: 8 servings

Ingredients:

2	(13-5 ounce) cans coconut milk
1/2	teaspoon vanilla extract
1/2	cup honey
1/2	cup mashed avocado
1/2	cup carob powder
1/2	teaspoon ground cinnamon (optional)

Directions:

1   In a medium saucepan, bring the coconut milk and vanilla to a boil. Reduce the heat and boil gently for 10 minutes, partially covered.

2   Remove the pan from the heat and whisk in the honey.

3   Carefully transfer the mixture to a blender and add the avocado, carob, and cinnamon. Blend on high until completely creamy. Pour into a glass bowl, cover with plastic wrap, and refrigerate until completely chilled, about 4 hours. Alternatively, to speed up the chilling process, pour the mixture into a sealed gallon-size plastic bag and submerge in an ice bath until completely chilled.

4   Pour the chilled mixture into an ice cream maker and mix until the ice cream has reached a thick soft-serve consistency. Freeze until firm, about 4 hours.

Desserts & Beverages

Ultra-Creamy Mint Ice Cream

The creamiest paleo ice cream I've tried, this is a delicious and refreshing summertime treat! The avocado gives it an ultra-creamy texture, and I promise you won't taste it.

Prep Time: 10 minutes   Cooking Time: 10 minutes

Chilling Time: 4-8 hours   Yield: 8 servings

Ingredients:

2   (13.5-ouce) cans coconut milk

1/2   teaspoon peppermint extract

1/2   teaspoon vanilla extract

1/2   cup honey

1/2   cup mashed avocado

1   small handful baby spinach (optional, for added color)

Directions:

1   In a medium saucepan, bring the coconut milk, peppermint extract, and vanilla to a boil. Reduce the heat and boil gently for 10 minutes, partially covered.

2   Remove from the heat and whisk in the honey.

3   Carefully transfer the mixture to a blender and add the avocado and spinach. Blend on high speed until completely creamy. Pour into a glass bowl, cover with plastic wrap, and refrigerate until completely chilled, about 4 hours. Alternatively, to speed up the chilling process, pour the mixture into a sealed gallon-size plastic bag and submerge in an ice bath until completely chilled.

4   Pour the chilled mixture into an ice cream maker and mix until the ice cream has reached a thick soft-serve consistency. Freeze until firm, about 4 hours.

Tips:

I often make green vanilla ice cream using this recipe by replacing the 1/2 teaspoon of peppermint extract with vanilla extract.

Chocolate Mousse–Stuffed Strawberries

These are a light and decadent treat, dessert, or fruit side to bring to a party or shower. To make them even easier to put together, you can slice them instead of filling them and serve the chocolate mousse as a dip!

 Prep Time: 15 minutes   Yield: 6 servings

Ingredients:

1	pound strawberries
1	large avocado, peeled and seeded
1/4	cup coconut milk
3	tablespoons carob powder
3	tablespoons honey
1/2	teaspoon ground cinnamon (optional)
	pinch sea salt

Directions:

1 Wash the strawberries and cut a cone-shaped hole into the tops of each one (removing the stem).

2 In a food processor or blender, blend the remaining ingredients until very smooth.

3 Pipe or spoon the filling into the strawberries. Chill until ready to serve.

Tea Latte

Coffee and coffee shops have been part of my everyday life since college. I used to go to bed thinking how good that morning cup of coffee would taste the next morning. Backing off of my beloved coffee was a real struggle, but these recipes help me fill that craving with delicious drinks!

🍴 Prep Time: 8 minutes   🎁 Yield: 2 servings

Ingredients:

12	ounces boiling water
1-2	tea bags (I recommend black or rooibos tea)
1/4	cup coconut cream or coconut milk
2	tablespoons honey

Directions:

1 Let the tea bags steep in the boiling water for 5 minutes. Meanwhile, place the remaining ingredients into a blender.

2 When finished steeping, add the hot tea to the blender. Blend on high speed until frothy.

Variations:

Vanilla Latte: Add 1 teaspoon vanilla extract to the water before boiling.

Caramel Machiatto: Instead of honey, use coconut palm sugar. Add 1/8 teaspoon of sea salt.

Pumpkin Spice Latte: Before blending, add 1/4 cup pumpkin purée, 1/8 teaspoon ground cinnamon, 1/8 teaspoon ground ginger, a pinch of ground cloves, and a pinch of ground mace.

Hot Cocoa

This hot cocoa is cocoa-less, but it fills the warm chocolaty craving just as beautifully!

Prep Time: 5 minutes   Yield: 4 servings

Ingredients:

2   (13.5-ounce) can coconut milk

3   tablespoons carob powder

1/4   cup maple syrup

1/2   teaspoon ground cinnamon

       pinch sea salt

Directions:

Whisk all the ingredients together in a medium saucepan. Heat until desired temperature is reached. This can also be made in a high-speed blender with heating capabilities.

Tips:

The crème filling from N'oatmeal Crème Pies (page 131) is wonderful to use as a marshmallow topping for this drink.

Desserts &
Beverages

Lemonade

Honey-sweetened and perfectly tart, this lemonade is a wonderfully refreshing treat!

Prep Time: 5 minutes   Yield: 4 servings

Ingredients:

2   cups hot water

1/2   cup honey

1   cup lemon juice, freshly-squeezed

       ice cubes

Directions:

Combine the honey and hot water in a pitcher. Stir until dissolved. Add the lemon juice and stir to combine. Cover and refrigerate until cool to the touch. Pour into glasses of ice to serve.

Gratitude

Without the many generous individuals who financially backed this project, this cookbook simply would not exist. A simple list of your printed names does not do justice to my gratitude for each one of you who believed in me and this project. Your generosity will help so many on their journey toward health and healing, and for you I am so thankful!

Mirra Bates
Betty Brooks
Larissa Clorley
Ernie and Hilary Dominguez
Mike and Sabrina Drewry
Julie Emmitt
Tracie L. Gonzalez
Kathy Gatten Johnson
Lynn Kloss
Teresa Emmitt LaFuze
Lisa Larson
AimeeMarie Lipat
Summer Lyons
Mary Manna
Amy Moore
Lynda O'Day
Kristy Powers
Rebecca Runo
Stacey Schuetze
Nils Smith
Kim Stewart
Heidi Tanninen
Nicole Taylor
Vicki Terronez
Roxanne Thurman
Mickey Trescott
Monica and Marc Wagenbach
Lori Wilburn
Terri Willeford
Beth Woolfolk
Tiffany Zwieg
Amy
Koala Bear

Chris, I'll say it now and forever more: there is no one on this entire earth I'd rather be married to. You're my best friend, my perfect counterpart, and you have relentlessly supported and cheered for every one of my (many) dreams. Thank you for being my guinea pig, even though you didn't realize it at the time. I love you so much.

My children, Daniel, David, Cara and Micah, Your compliments and never-ending praise of my food are my constant encourage-

ment. God outdid himself when he made each one of you, and I am so thankful I get to have you as my children. Also, thanks for helping load, unload, and load again the dishwasher multiple times a day. You all make the best dish and silverware sorters around. Micah, while you can't be seen in any of these photos, I take great joy in knowing you were being knit together in the beginning of pregnancy when these photos were taken. I love the four of you more than I could ever express!

Amy, You are one of the few people who knew what was going on when I felt my worst, and you were there by my side through each step of the healing journey. You've been such a great friend, recipe tester and honest critic. I'm so glad God made us neighbors.

Mama E, You didn't get to see the final product before you went to heaven. You were my greatest confidante and will always be the person I aspire to be just like. I can't wait until I see you again. Until then, save me a few gluten-filled rolls - I plan on eating a lot of those when I get to heaven one day.

To my parents: Thank you for allowing me to always explore my creativity and for putting up with my many messes in the kitchen. It looks like it may have finally paid off!

To my in-laws and extended family: Thank you for your unwavering support. I know there must have been times when you thought I was crazy for eating this way, but you've never said so and have always made sure I have food to eat at holiday dinners.

To Josh Huskin, Nicole Basci, Jennifer Hicks, Sarah Jane Jones, and Tracie Gonzalez: Your photography, marketing, design and editing skills are what turned this book from a mom-and-pop project to a professional and beautiful work. Thank you for your hard work, dedication and for being so fun to work with!

My heavenly Father, when I think about this journey, I can't help but marvel at all you've taught me in just a few short years. Thank you for sustaining me and pointing me toward the direction that gave me my life back. And just like in 2 Corinthians 1:4, I'm so thankful I can now use this as a positive experience to help others. Thank you.

Gingerbread House Template

for the use with the recipe on page 136.

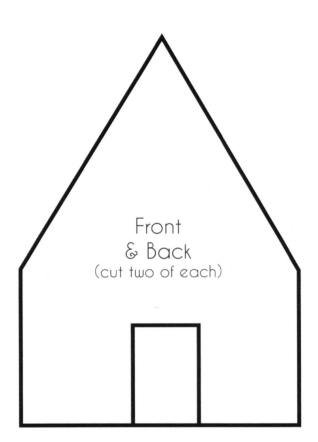

Front
& Back
(cut two of each)

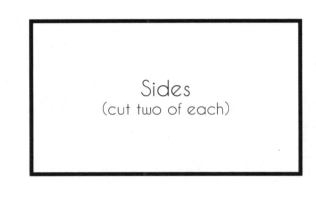

Sides
(cut two of each)

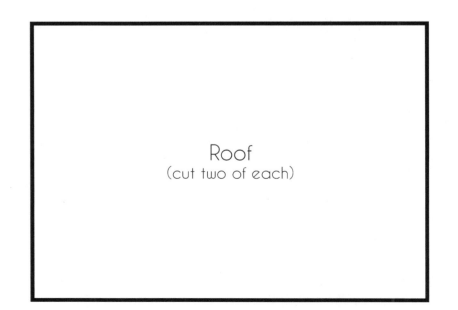

Roof
(cut two of each)

Index

Made in the USA
Middletown, DE
19 November 2016